You're Welcome, Mama
Permission Granted to be a Better You

By Dr. Heather Cook

To mamas out there wanting to get life right for their kiddos, I hope you find guidance through this book to give yourself permission to make moments happen.

To my daughter, I hope I show you a true spirit of loving, learning, and living so you can have the courage to change the world.

To my husband, I hope your pursuit (and achievement) of excellence shows Piper the value of hard work and the ability to tackle the impossible. You've shown that to me through your love of music and your love of me.

ACKNOWLEDGMENTS

So many people have helped me in this journey.
Below are a few who went the extra mile.
Thank you... from this Mama.

SHOUT OUT TO MY AWESOME MAMAS...

Dr. Jennifer Axsom Adler • Jeanette Blazier • Tara Burns • Claudia Byrd
Megan Christian • Etta Clark • Keely Goodwin • Anne Greenfield • Julie Gunn
Mikki Hale • Tara Hodges • Chrissy Idlette • Melissa Steagall-Jones • Julie Keeton
Katie Kerns • Michelle Mitchell • Deborah Mullins • Kristen Reedy • Pam Rehart
Jennifer Salyer • Ambre Torbett • Brenda White-Wright • Amanda Harvey Yampolski

SHOUT OUT TO MY AWESOME PEOPLE...

Anne Adamson • Adrienne Batara • Vanessa Bennett • Joy Carter • David Cate
Dr. John E. Cook • Kennon Cook • Morgan Cook • Pam Cox • Samantha Culbertson
Eric Deaton • Dr. Louise Dickson • Dr. Nancy Dishner • Darrell Duncan
Sharon Duncan • Dr. Brittney Ezell • Jeff Fleming • Kylee Fleming • Sarah Fleming
Phillis Fortney • David Golden • Shirley Grindstaff • Earl Grindstaff • Heath Guinn
Candi Harker • Roy Harmon • Alex Hayes • June Holder • Roy Holder
Autumn Hoover • Becky Jones • Bob Jones • Abby Keeton • Avery Keeton
Easton Keeton • Ellie Keeton • Emery Keeton • Kinley Keeton • Sutton Keeton
Karen Lovelace • Bobbie Phillips • Dennis Phillips • Bonnie Macdonald
Renee McBryar • Roger Mowen • Beverley Perdue • Mike Rehart • Curt Rose
Michael Rosales • Margot Seay • Becky Schamore • Ryan Shipley • Ashley Shutt
Jessica Slaughter • Lisa Templeton • Lynn Tully • Marcy Walker • Keith Wilson
Melissa Woods • and many more to come...

TABLE OF CONTENTS

PART I: I'M OVERWHELMED

Chapter 1: Journey
Don't Go to School Naked

Chapter 2: Time
Dog or Daughter - Pick One

Chapter 3: Stress
They Think I'm Crazy

PART II: I'M JUST SURVIVING

Chapter 4: Failing
Crying Makes My Skin Crawl

Chapter 5: Desensitized
I'm Hungry... I'm Scared... I Need a Hug... I Need to Pee

Chapter 6: Grumpy
I am NOT Wonder Woman - I am Me

PART III: WHAT'S HAPPENING TO ME

Chapter 7: Civility
I Don't Love You Right Now

Chapter 8: Awareness
Mama, Why is She So Fat

Chapter 9: Filter
Your Sinus Infection Makes Me Want to Punch You

PART IV: I CAN DO THIS

Chapter 10: Character
Mud Makes it Better

Chapter 11: Balance
Extreme Good Comes from Balance

Chapter 12: Motivation
When are We Gonna Start Dancing

PART V: HERE WE GO

Chapter 13: Think
Unicorns are Real... Sometimes

Chapter 14: Connection
You Have a Lot of Homework

Chapter 15: Exceed Expectations
Piper is Ready

INTRODUCTION

The Thoughts in My Head

I kept noticing two glaring moments where I thought mamas were trying too hard.

One - those mamas who feel compelled to seem like they have it all together on social media with the perfect family photo or the latest kid achievement. They compete with other moms, relentlessly pursuing social acceptance. And for what real gain?

Two - mamas forget about themselves and constantly wonder why they are tired, frustrated, and a little crazy. They need to learn to be good to themselves so they can be good to others. They hide their vulnerabilities to the point that the only one to crumble is mama.

I wanted to take these thoughts and put them into actionable things mamas could easily implement into their daily routine.

So I did. You're Welcome, Mama.

Heather Cook, the Mama

I grew up without my biological mama, so I found myself constantly seeking teachers, neighbors, and strangers to be my mama. I was raised by two wonderful grandparents, my mama's parents, who are the reason I turned out okay. I was always surrounded by love (and wouldn't change a thing), yet I must have had a small hole in my heart left by my real mama, because I kept trying to fill it.

When I became a mama, I wanted to make sure I was doing everything right, everything possible so that I could always be my daughter's mama. Every time I messed up, I worried that someone would think I wasn't fit to keep my baby. That was silly. I know better. Yet, I think many mamas have similar feelings of wanting to get it right and thinking they are not.

No pity needed here. I am thankful for my life, how I was raised, and how I turned out. The ebb and flows in my life led me to where I am today, and I'm thankful.

As a mama, I wanna love. Love people. Love experiences. Love things. Love the world. Love moments.

1

I love to dance, even though my moves are not as good as they used to be. I love to sing out loud, and I think I have wonderful intonation and inflection. Ha! I love to eat at cool restaurants where I can't pronounce everything on the menu, and I love to travel to new places. My husband and I take our daughter somewhere new every year so she can experience all kinds of things. I love homemade vanilla ice cream topped with extra Nutella and fresh strawberries. I love to sit on the back porch and listen to music and smile. I love to help my daughter try new things. And, I really love watching mamas be good to themselves. Permission granted to go and be awesome!

You're welcome, Mama.

The Light Bulb Moment

I wrote this book to share with all young mamas that "You've Got This!" I want my stories, my failures, my crazy moments, and my triumphs to be a small snapshot that resonates with what most mamas deal with. Mamas need someone in their life constantly giving them permission to be good to themselves. They deserve it.

I was sitting in a cozy, coffee shop one morning with some mamas trying to sort through a bunch of titles for my book. We had been there about an hour, and I was starting to feel bummed that we couldn't find the right one to connect to the purpose of the book.

All of a sudden, one of the mamas looked at me, and said, "I've got it!" She went on to recount the story about when she first read my manuscript. She shared a time when she sent me a really, really long text thanking me for letting her read the book. She told the mamas she wrote, "I would never have done this for myself. You gave me permission to be good to myself."

Voila - there's my title: You're Welcome, Mama: Permission Granted to be a Better You.

This book is my gift to mamas.

I know how I felt, and still feel sometimes, as a mama trying to get it all right. I want to share my stories and encourage other mamas to be good to themselves. It will make them better mamas for sure.

How to Read this Book

This book is intended to be whatever you need it to be. I wrote it because I find many women try to hide their vulnerabilities, actions which keep them from overcoming them. I wanted mamas to know that we all have these, what seem to be, universal moments we try and tackle alone. No matter what part of the roller coaster you're on, someone is there with you and gets it. This book is real. This book is funny (I hope). This book will get you on your way to creating the life you deserve.

We often don't give ourselves permission to be good to ourselves. Baby first. Kids first. Others first. If we ever allow ourselves some "me time," we end up feeling guilty. I hope this book inspires you to do something for yourself because it will make you a *better* person, not a selfish one. My sole purpose in writing this book was to grant permission to other mamas, because we will never give that permission to ourselves.

Each chapter has a theme with a story included, a story that happened and is real. I'm guessing most mamas can relate.

Each chapter starts with an old adage that connects to the theme. After each story, I provide my own, updated adage that seems way more applicable to today's crazy life!

Finally, at the end of each chapter, I include a challenge and action items to support each theme. The challenges are memorable and the action items are bite-sized, which means everything that speaks to you can be added to your life in a reasonable way.

This book can be a light-hearted read that makes you laugh and brightens your day. It can serve as a resource, depending on your stage of motherhood and what problems you're currently tackling. It can be a constant reminder that no matter how far you've come in your journey, you may get kicked back down to survival mode from time to time. You can also take each chapter at your own pace and diligently implement the challenge and action items to become a better you, the real you.

This book, hopefully, is something you will refer to as a nice refresher. Just like a good professional development session to re-energize you, sometimes, you just need permission to do something for yourself.

Everyone benefits.

The Gap

The gap is between what you want and what you get. Unfortunately, many mamas persist in this gap. The purpose of this book is to take you on a journey from "I can't even..." to "I'm ready for more..." Wherever we are in life, we *all* could use a little nudge and a little humor sprinkled throughout our days.

But how do we actually do it? How do we get there? We already want more out of life, but rarely do we get there.

Great advice surrounds us. Why can't we accept it? Why can't we change? Some say we're hard wired not to change, and some say we're too busy. Excuses are never in short supply. Permission is *always* in short supply.

I think it's because change is uncomfortable. It's uncomfortable for you and for others around you. Take for instance, trying to lose weight. You're cranky because you're eating less and that affects everyone around you. The doctor says you're on the verge of a heart attack, but you really, really love steak. Should you be cranky and eat better because your life depends on it? Yes. It just pushes you out of your comfort zone.

Your boss gives you a poor performance review, yet he hadn't said anything to date of your inability to complete a task. That's because it was uncomfortable to tell you.

The lists are endless as to why we have this gap, and we always find a reason not to close the gap. It's either too hard, too messy, or we're really not motivated yet.

Most of the time, we have not reached a place where we feel it's so uncomfortable that it's actually worse *not* to change. When our consequence (fear of dying) exceeds our behaviors (start healthy habits), then we can start to close the gap.

Closing the Gap

Self-help books. Counseling. Alcohol. Yoga. So many methods. While there are successes, there is no secret. You just have to decide you want to close the gap. No one can make you. Just knowing you need to, that's not enough. You've got to really want to. And then, you've gotta have someone who will give you permission to work on yourself. And most importantly, *YOU* must be the one to give yourself permission to close the gap, to be better. Good luck!

Part 1:
I'm Overwhelmed

CHAPTER 1: JOURNEY

The journey of a thousand miles begins with one step.

Don't Go to School Naked

I was at a conference, taking full advantage that opening session wasn't until 9:00 that morning. There I was, in my nice comfy hotel bed, sleeping late for the first time in, well, I can't remember how long. It was a fancy hotel where the sheets were cool and soft – a perfect place to sleep.

Then, I got a text from my husband. I thought, "Really? He knew this was my one morning to indulge."

It was a video of my daughter, Piper. Instead of the anticipated cute "Piper going to school" video, I got footage of a screaming, naked, crazy child refusing to put on clothes.

My early-rising streak continued. I wanted one day. Just *one day* to sleep in. Instead, my child had turned into a little baby demon.

My first thought (which my husband quickly recognized) was, "You really can't handle one morning? Just. One. Morning?"

Like a good mama, I FaceTimed and tried to talk to the little devil. Her eyes were swollen, and she was screaming that her head hurt. I thought, "Well duh." I tried all the calming, soothing, "mommy is really nice" tricks, and nothing worked. My sweet husband looked at me in the selfie position and said, "See, I literally have no idea what to do."

Piper was three.

It was the day of Piper's first-ever field trip (let's not mention the guilt of missing this first). She was going to a pumpkin patch at a local farm. Each kiddo would get to pick out his or her very own pumpkin to bring home. Piper was so excited and kept saying that she did, in fact, want to go to the pumpkin patch, just not with clothes on. Kids and their need for nakedness. Ugh.

Then, in my still comatose state, an idea popped into my brain. I said to my husband, "Baby, go put her in the car with no clothes on, and tell her she has to go to school... naked." At his wits end, he must have thought that was his only option. He said, "I'll call you right back." He did not evaluate if I might have been joking or if our daughter might be scarred forever; he just needed another option.

With her arms flailing, kicking and screaming, my husband carried Piper with his arms straight out like something was dripping, or in this case, a little crazy person that could cause damage to your face and kidneys.

Meanwhile, I was patiently awaiting the verdict. Did it work? I had just given my husband the craziest idea. Was he really putting our three-year-old daughter in the car naked? I was joking, wasn't I? Geez, my poor mama advice was being executed. I thought, "Oh dear."

My husband called back in about ten minutes and said, "Wow, thank you! That worked! I put her in the car seat naked. I even buckled her! And guess what? She said crying, 'Daddy please, I don't want to go to school naked! I promise I'll put clothes on.'"

Well, Mom and Dad of the year. Good or bad, you decide. If you have kids, you'll likely think we were brilliant. If you don't have kids, you may not read beyond this sentence.

Long story short - Piper wanted something (field trip), but didn't want to do what it took to get there (put clothes on). Count the number of times you've wanted something and didn't really want to do what it took to get there.

A few quick examples of my own:
- I want to lose 20 pounds, but I don't want to eat better. Food is joyful.
- I want to run a 5k, but I can't find time to exercise, much less train.
- I want to be in better financial shape, but I'm not good at math, and I love experiences now, not later. (Instant gratification is going to kill us. Check out my next book one day on that one.)
- I want my child to be extra smart, but I decide a little (okay, a lot) of TV can't be that bad. Some shows are even educational.

We have lots of wants. We like goals. We know goals are good for us. They provide motivation and purpose. Then, we by God, kick and scream and need someone else to have an intervention with us before we actually make any progress.

In order to work toward a goal, **our consequence must exceed our behavior.** For Piper, going to school naked was worse than putting on clothes. For me, buying a whole new wardrobe is worse than losing 20 pounds. Well, I say that, yet I did buy a bunch of cool shawls and leggings, for the meantime.

The journey ~~of a~~ X thousand
miles begins with one step.

Put clothes on before leaving
the house.

CHALLENGE: Close the gap.

Life takes you in so many directions. It's hard to know if you are
even on a journey or if you're living in this chaotic minute-to-minute
survival mode where you crash at night, and the only relief is from 1
a.m. to 4 a.m. when you actually sleep.

It's important to take a step in the direction of knowing what you
want. What makes you happy? What energizes you? Where do you find
satisfaction?

Develop a worthy journey around the answers to those questions.
In order to close the gap, we have to make an effort to work
on ourselves. It's hard to get started, but once you do, small
improvements can make a difference in your attitude.

I encourage you to give yourself permission to...

1. START SMALL.

Don't try and reclaim it all at once. Make a mini goal. Do it for a week. Enjoy the fleeting satisfaction of completing your goal for two weeks (the average time required to change a habit). Then, make it a lifetime decision. Then, remind yourself that lifestyle change is satisfying for longer than a minute.

Repeat with another mini goal.

Soon enough, you will have created journeys in your life that provide meaning to moments. For example, start with drinking more water. That's all, something itty-bitty, something achievable. Start with saying, "We'll see," with your kids instead of an instant "No."

2. CREATE VISIBLE REMINDERS.

What do you enjoy doing? Jot down a few things on a notepad. Post them in your office, on the fridge, or on your bathroom mirror. This is a simple and friendly reminder to think about things you enjoy. It's amazing how a reminder can prompt you to actually do something you want to do. Things you are supposed to do will always get in the way, if you allow them to.

It's up to you to take five minutes (or a full Saturday) to do something about it. Trust me. If you have a family, you'll likely experience an entire guilt phase associated with doing something you want to, just because you want to. It's okay. You will be a better wife, mother, sister, colleague, and friend if you give this time to yourself. Give yourself permission to be better by getting to Chapter 2. It's about finding time you don't think you have.

3. GET UP EARLIER.

That's when most people really have extra time. Then again, I hate the thought of this, so just act like I never said it. Getting up earlier is like 4:00 a.m.! (If you're naturally a morning person, I will do my best to still like you.)

Okay, so here's the real #3 (because overworked, exhausted people do not want to be chipper at 5 a.m.).

3. UNDERSTAND SATISFACTION.

When satisfaction is fleeting, I would argue you didn't really experience it. **Satisfaction should last.** If it doesn't, you may want to take a look at what brings you such fleeting satisfaction. Raising a child takes at least 18 years. That's an overwhelming task. Find milestones to work toward, so you can appreciate wins along the way. No need to fret about your children becoming adults when there are thousands of moments before that happens.

CHAPTER 2: TIME

The best things in life are free.

DOG OR DAUGHTER - PICK ONE

There I was sitting at my computer, like a zombie, staring at my screen. I felt paralyzed. It was Thursday at 3:40 p.m., and my chance at productivity was rapidly fading. Instead of trying to knock out a couple of tasks, I just sat there, zoned out because I couldn't even figure out what to do next.

Ever felt like that? Yep, often.

All of a sudden: bing, buzz, ring. All my devices were yelling at me to go to a meeting. I say yelling because it's like I was mad at them for making me snap out of my zombie moment. Lord, I can't even be thankful they broke my temporarily paralyzed brain. Ugh, what a day!

So off to my meeting I went. Guess what happened at this meeting? My to-do list got longer. I felt my neck tighten, and my jaw started to ache. Oh boy. How in the world was I going to get any of this done by tomorrow?

Meeting is over. Work day is over. Wow, what an unproductive couple of hours. At least there's a small silver lining. The meeting ended on time, and I get to pick up my daughter at daycare before 5:29 p.m. Victory - she's not the last kiddo to be picked up today!

To celebrate my minor victory, I turn up the music and start singing to Disney's *Where You Are* from Moana.[1] Of course, it is what's already playing in the car, and I know every word.

Moana...
Make way! Make way!
Moana it's time you knew... the village of Motunui... is all you need.
The dancers are practicing. Ah ha.
They dance to an ancient song. Oh ho.

Then the phone rings and shuts down my toddler jam. It's the groomer. As soon as I see the number, I know why they are calling. Dang it! My dog, Sophie, is at the groomer. The nice lady on the other end of the line reminds me Sophie is still (ahem) at the groomer, and she needs to be picked up by 5:30 p.m.

Both my dog and daughter must be picked up by 5:30 p.m.

Which one do I pick up? Dog or daughter?

I'm driving down the road and contemplating dog or daughter. Seriously, this is my day.

I'm getting to the split in the road. I cannot think normally because I have a ridiculous decision in front of me and now, the split.

Left takes me to the groomer. Right takes me to daycare.

And..

I choose my dog.

Who am I? What kind of mama am I? Well, before you judge me (if you haven't already), I had a valid reason.

Here's the logic. If I don't pick up my dog by 5:30 p.m., my dog has to stay all night in a cage, and I have to pay for that.

If I don't pick my daughter up by 5:30 p.m., she does not have to spend all night at daycare, and definitely not in a cage, and I only owe $10 for being late.

So, see... I made a reasonable decision at the end of the day to pick up both of my children.

Think about the days where you contemplate random, unplanned, obnoxious decisions because you don't have time to get it done any faster; it's just what happened to be thrown on your plate. We feel we don't have enough time, and I'm pretty sure these days are common. Ultra-productive or relaxing days – not so common.

What's your crazy, random, forced choice?

Dog or daughter?
Spouse or boss?
Salad or donut?

We all have our own dog or daughter scenario, and it makes for a great story later, as I hope you've enjoyed. Yet in the moment, it makes you feel crazy, like you can't handle your life.

Mamas, it's all about the time you have and how you spend it.

Time is the ultimate equalizer. Other people may have more education or more experience. Other people may have more money or more connections. EVERYONE has the same 24 hours in their day. In order to create more time, you must create more space. Productivity demands you find more time. How are you using your 24 hours?

The best things ~~in~~ life are free.

free is cheap. Be better
than that.

CHALLENGE: CREATE SPACE, NOT WASTE.

How many times have you gotten nothing done because you have so much to do you cannot decide where to start? When you're paralyzed by the fact you know you're not going to get it all done, what do you do? You shut down. It's so easy to create waste in your life and not even realize it. It's important to know the difference between a break and waste.

Becoming more aware of your day's realities will allow you to prioritize your to-do list and get on it!

Let's list a few items that suck time out of your day: emails, social media, your open office door, celebrity gossip shows, cat videos. You get the picture.

Permission granted to give these a try...

1. Stop "Blaahking."

Here's a new word for you. I made it up. You're welcome and encouraged to use it. It's essentially word-vomit, and it's what we do on social media. We scan a headline, a friend's viewpoint and then, boom- we embark on a social media rant with a thought based on little to no research. All you did was "blaahk." "Blaahking" typically starts a rant of more regurgitated words, and soon enough you've "blaahked" all over social media for the world to see. Embarrassing.

I especially hate those who lead with, "I don't typically do this but..." or "Please don't comment. I just want to rant." Malarky.

For all of you who are "blaahking" out there, add that up, and think about how much space you could have created.

2. End your day with a list.

Why? Most people start their day with a list, which takes up time that you could have been productive. End your day with a list of what you accomplished, not just a list for tomorrow. Taking a couple of minutes and writing out what you completed for the day gives a sense of accomplishment. Then, write your to-do list for tomorrow, which will allow you to rest better and be ready to tackle the next day.

This list should also include "four rooms" you need to enter each day, which you will learn about below.

3. Walk into four rooms.

There's a Native American Proverb that references how to become a whole being. Native Americans strongly feel you must walk into four rooms each day in order to be whole. The four rooms are physical, mental, emotional, and spiritual.

Giving yourself time to walk into each room boosts your productivity and attitude. Being intentional about each room gives you space. You did something for you. If you don't think you have this time, next time you're mindlessly scrolling social media, stop and do something meaningful. Mindfulness is the new professional development. We're so bombarded by information that the volume and pace is not manageable. We must be intentional about "sitting on the back porch" like people used to. We have so much coming at us that we need time to process, time to reflect. We can only truly accomplish that if we are mindful.

Here are some quick and simple examples of how to walk into each room, each day. Some days, quick is all you have. Other days, GO BIG.

Physical - Obviously, exercise. If you're like me, it's definitely not daily and happens more like once every couple of weeks, if I'm lucky. Take a multivitamin. Drink water. Choose a healthy snack. For those new mamas, get a shower. And my favorite - GO BIG and run a 5K and then, go get a massage!

Mental - Read two opposing articles just to learn. Play brain games (free apps), or GO BIG and learn a new language, starting with a few words per day.

Emotional - Listen to music you enjoy. For example, think about an emotional movie and how much the music added to the moments. Do something kind for someone else. GO BIG and keep reading this book and apply it to your daily life!

Spiritual - Pray. Meditate. Find your source of spirituality that allows you to feel complete. Be still. Take in the awe of this world and all its living things. GO BIG and do a multi-day spiritual challenge for renewal and reflection.

CHAPTER 3: STRESS

A bird in the hand is worth two in the bush.

THEY THINK I'M CRAZY

Think about how bottled up passive-aggressiveness can explode on you at an insignificant time, thus embarrassing you and making you look crazy. Let's try and fix this.

Think about it. Something bothers you. You bottle it. Something bugs you. You let it slide. Something else gets to you. You let it go. At some point, these little incidences add up until you can no longer be silent. Then, you spew. You spew word vomit at loud decibels that prompt people to give you a what-the-hell look. You may add crying, bold hand gestures, and unintentional spitting. Yep, that kind of spewing.

I think about a Christmas that started a slight unraveling of my family. In addition to the "normal" holiday stress, my grandmother (who raised me) had a stroke, and she came to live with me for a few days. My husband got shingles on his face and in his eye. Then, in addition to shingles, he got kidney stones. The ER sent him home thinking he had back spasms. My dad had an ulcerative colitis flare up, which landed him in the hospital, and my stepmom's dad was hospitalized for C-Diff. (Google that. Yuck.) This all occurred in a concentrated period of barely three weeks.

I tried my best to handle the stress. I was the glue holding it all together. Managing doctor appointments, picking up prescriptions from multiple pharmacies for multiple people, rearranging schedules, handling a toddler - I was the glue. I had no choice but to be strong and get things done. All mamas have been there. No permission to do anything for ourselves because there is always something more important than whatever it is we want (or need) to do.

Luckily, I had a business trip scheduled, which included one day for me to escape and get away from the stress. I was going to take full advantage!

But then... One. More. Thing. Happened.

I'm boarding the plane to come home, feeling refreshed and ready to tackle my next set of challenges, be what they may.

Then my grandmother, mind you who had just had a stroke, called to say in her slow, Southern drawl, "Weeelllll, Heaaaather, I guess I should go ahead and tell ya that I fell down all of my steps on Friday and broke my shoulder."

This was Sunday! She had been sitting and sleeping on the couch for two days!

Guilt set in.

My day, the one day I had given myself, is now full of guilt. Dammit.

And out came my active passive aggressiveness! Here we go...

I have a 3 ½ hour flight back to continue my self-inflicted guilt. I also want to be angry. She should have told me. In her words, she wanted me to travel and didn't dare want me to stay home for her. Gosh, should I still be thankful? All of these thoughts are running through my brain.

Also in my brain, is my firm commitment to order the fruit and cheese plate when the flight attendant gets to me. I've been trying to make better choices (it's January - entirely too early to give up on my New Year's resolution), so I'm choosing fruit and cheese instead of Biscoff cookies. Big step for me!

Right before the lady gets to me, the first class flight attendant walks back and asks my flight attendant for a fruit and cheese plate from her cart. She gives her one. Then, I'm next. I say, "I'd like to get one of those fruit and cheese plates too, please." The lady looks at me and pauses. Then she says, "Oh dear. I'm so sorry, but that was the last one."

Blink. Blink.

My eyes are stinging. The last three weeks come rushing out of me like a rabid animal. I cannot take it anymore. Yep, I'm going to spew on this lady.

My spew came without thought, in warp speed.

"But that was MYYYYYY fruit and cheese plate! You gave away MYYYYYY fruit and cheese!"

Yes, others start to look at me, and I finally stop saying "MY fruit and cheese" over and over. I move on to, "Why did you do it? Why do you carry so few fruit and cheese plates? Just because I'm in the back, doesn't mean I don't have a right to eat fruit and cheese, too!"

I'm running out of breath because I've talked so fast and literally must take a breath.

The flight attendant, trying to deal with me, asks if I would like to have anything else on the menu.

I look at her puzzled and say at about 350 words per minute, "No, no, no! I only wanted fruit and cheese, and you gave away my fruit and cheese; therefore, there is nothing left for me. I am trying to be good. It's January. Every female tries to be good at least through January. So, the only thing on your menu that is remotely healthy is fruit and cheese. I needed fruit and cheese. I'm trying to be good and only wanted a fruit and cheese plate. If I can't have fruit and cheese, I'll go without. Fewer calories anyway. Thank you."

Then, I lean back in my chair and close my eyes and a tear runs down my cheek. I am done.

We all have these "lose it and regret it" moments. The flight attendant likely went back to her friends and unloaded this hilarious story about this passenger who lost it over fruit and cheese. She likely made fun of me and had a good laugh at my expense. That's fair. I did seem crazy. What she didn't know was the previous three weeks of my life. No one on the plane had a clue.

Do people really know how you're doing if you are holding it all in? Can you be vulnerable, or should you be? Must you be tough, or is it okay to vent or cry or whatever emotion seems most relevant at the time?

We mamas stay strong way more often, which only builds the chance of spewing craziness on someone at any given moment.

A bird in the ~~hand~~ is worth two in the bush.

If a bird in the hand poops on you, go wash it off, and be glad it didn't poke your eye out.

CHALLENGE: COMPARTMENTALIZE YOUR CRAP.

Deal with what matters and don't let your emotions spill over into areas where they are not relevant. You had a bad work day; don't bring it home. Your kid got in trouble at school; don't let it ruin the rest of your day.

If you're going to handle your emotions better, you need to compartmentalize your crap. You need to put things into perspective, and not allow one round of crap to start seeping into another part of your life that's functioning just fine.

The end is more important than the beginning. It's also more memorable.[2] What you take with you each day is something that wowed you, embarrassed you, or stung you. Rarely do you recount the everyday minutia. It's forgettable. Your journey will be made up of these crazy moments. Count on it. Compartmentalize those yucky ones and focus on something that's actually working.

Moments, good and bad, create who you are. You are defined by moments in your life. Do your best to multiply wow moments for others and limit those moments that sting. If we're only going to remember endings and extremes, isn't it worth making them matter?

Permission granted to compartmentalize your crap into manageable boxes so it doesn't consume you and everyone around you.

A bad start can end just fine if you allow it.

Permission granted to give these a try...

1. SCREAM.

Yes, scream. Do it alone with vigor or silently when no one is looking.
Typically, I do the one where you clench fists and jaws and shake.
No real sound comes out, but if you were watching me on mute, you
would definitely think I was screaming. It provides a much-needed
release.

2. TAKE A BREAK

We used to unwind after work until the next day. Now, we work 24/7
because we allow access to everyone via our phone. Schedule that
break.

I recommend two five-minute breaks during the work day, and this
does not mean a break to check your email. If you're at a full-day
seminar, 99% of the people use their break to catch up on work stuff.
Therefore, they didn't really give themselves a break. No wonder your
brain is tired. Now, to make sure you take a real break, you need to
physically add breaks into your calendar. Then, don't delete them or
ignore them.

Even if it's just five minutes, you need a break to handle the next five
hours. Take a lap around your office or around the block. Check that
box for the Physical Room - one of your four rooms to walk in each
day. If you don't have space to walk, then try bathroom squats. Yep,
do a quick ten squats in the bathroom, and it's a little mini boost for
your day. Here's a mini goal!

If you are unable to leave where you are at the time, then just
breathe. Yes, there is a reason that pops up on default mode if you
have an Apple Watch. You need it. Its default setting reminds you
to breathe and stand. Lordy, what's happening to us that we need a
device to tell us to do something that is supposed to be involuntary? It
speaks to the fact we must be reminded to do basic human functions
we will not automatically do for ourselves.

3. REAPPRAISE.

Take a look at a negative or disappointing situation after it happens. Then, find a new lens. It will reduce your stress and allow you to move forward. Lose a loved one? Grieve in your own way, and then take that loss and do something meaningful in memory of your loved one. Lose a job? A better fit is out there for you. Had a bad day? Fix it by drinking the bottle instead of a glass. This one particularly helps me. (Disclaimer: Don't really do this. I'm told it can be seen as "unhealthy.")

PART 11:
I'M JUST SURVIVING

CHAPTER 4: FAILING

No Pain. No Gain.

CRYING MAKES MY SKIN CRAWL

Babies cannot tell you what they want. After multiple hours of not being able to tell you what they want, they scream. It's all they know to do when you cannot figure out what they want. All mamas have been there. We look at our crying baby and blame them. Why won't you quit crying? I've fed you, I've rocked you, and I've been happy and nice to you, yet you still scream at me. At some point, crying makes my skin crawl.

How many times have you felt not equipped to mom? You're just so tired, and all you want is for your baby to stop crying.

One night, I was home alone, and Piper was on hour three of crying. I'm pretty sure crying becomes grating after ten minutes. I was on my 18th ten-minute dose (if my math is right). I was trying to put Piper down, and her face was red from wailing. I didn't know what to do. I'd run the gamut of options.

I had no reasonable options left. I was done.

I picked her up from the crib, and she let out this blood-curdling scream as if to say, "Why in the world did I get you as a mother? You're awful at this!"

My response (now remember, I'm done) was this:

I glared at her and tightened my hands. I was holding her over the crib, and I screamed (not what I meant when I said "scream" in Chapter 3) back at her, "Why won't you stop crying? Stop it! Stop crying!" I then proceeded to lay her down, leave her bawling, and went into my bedroom and started bawling, too.

Don't worry. A sweet friend came over and knew to check the toes. She instantly stopped crying. I had no idea she had a hair wrapped around her toe - and people, that is a serious issue in case you didn't know. For real.

There's always a good reason why they cry as babies. We just don't always know it. There's not always a good reason why *we* cry.
We all have these moments. If you cannot relate, you are likely in serious denial or have postpartum hypomania - it's real, too.

While a newborn is a worthy exhaustion, exhaustion messes with you. When you cannot remember the last time you bathed or brushed your teeth, you start doing some weird stuff in delirium.

I'm convinced kiddos don't remember much before age three, because they would be scarred by some of the things we did and didn't mean to do. God knew this and protected our kiddos!

Permission granted to fail, fail hard. It's the best way to appreciate the good stuff.

No pain. X No gain.

Real pain. Real gain.

CHALLENGE: LET IT GO.

While Disney's *Frozen* popularized these three words, their meaning reigns true. With that said, I would like to argue if Elsa and Anna were THAT close, then they never would have gone years without seeing each other in their own house, and they would have shared all of their secrets. I think girls are much smarter than that. Nonetheless, Elsa "let it go," and she felt free. You should do the same.

What good is failure doing if you let it weigh you down? The point is to learn from it. Looking back, my best experiences came out of failures. That's when I grew the most, even if I didn't like it or it was painful. When I didn't do something well or was in a bad situation, I learned *who* I didn't want to be, and *what* I didn't want to do. You have to have failures to fully appreciate successes.

I want Piper to fail. Then, I want her to let it go. Then, I want her to have the confidence to go after whatever she wants. I need to let her do this, not because it's easy to watch, but because it's good for character development.

There is value in pain. There is value in growing pains. There is newfound respect for gain, once you've felt pain.

Permission granted to give these a try...

1. OWN YOUR FAILURE.

On a scale from 1-10, how bad is it? Work to bring it closer to 0. Think about how much that failure will matter in five minutes or five days or five years. Don't let anything weigh on you past five years, no matter how traumatic. This does not dismiss grief as it's part of the process. You must eventually find a way to take tragedy and move forward.

- Bad parenting moment? You should be able to own that failure (actually, rationalize it, feel guilty about it, and then let it go) in five minutes. In reality, it may take you five days to really forgive yourself.

- Bad career move? This is one that's harder to own. However, it's not as daunting as you might think. It's not an immediate fix, but you should be able to own this failure in less than five years. In reality, it may take you longer if you don't have the confidence to be bold and change career paths. Many people feel stuck, like they don't have the education or the experience to jump ship and try something new. Then again, the working world is moving toward independent contractors where everyone is his or her own boss. Corporations reduce overhead this way, and individuals can create an amazing amount of flexibility in their schedules. Be bold and don't let the wrong path keep you from jumping to the right one.

- Or even worse, a bad partner move? This is one you can deal with in five years, but you won't. Counseling, faith, comfort, and lots of shared memories makes it tough to even consider another option. In reality, it's going to take you much longer than five years to own this failure. In fact, you may not even realize the true nature of your relationship until close to five years into it. Honeymoon periods can last a long time. Reality always comes in at some point, good or bad. No matter which way you cut it, if you're in a bad relationship, it's going to take longer than you think to get out of it. It's going to be messy. No way around it.

- Bad health habits? You're doing nothing to own this failure. In fact, it doesn't even register because your consequence has yet to exceed your behavior. Unless you're motivated, you likely will not even realize you need to deal with this failure until twenty plus years down the road, when it may be too late.

Find a way to quickly diagnose the true pains or realities from your failures. Then, work to move on. Don't let grief, doubt, guilt, and other negative emotions weigh you down from working toward conquering them.

The happiest people learn to deal. It doesn't mean they haven't experienced real tragedy. Trust me, they have. They just don't let it paralyze them.

2. BE THE ONE.

There are so few people who are willing to change and grow from their failings. We mamas should be that teeny-tiny percent that get it done.

Research suggests we really cannot change.

For example, in a 2018 Rotary International article, a study revealed seven heart attack patients whose doctors told them they must change their habits or they would soon die.[3] That's sobering information. How many do you think changed their habits?

One.

Why will we not do what we know is good for us? Are we really that stubborn? There are books, conventions, consultants, preachers, and more out there in this world advocating for change. Change is hard, especially complex (and must-be-motivated-in-order-to-actually-do-it) change. We must try - for not trying means no progress.

3. FIND A QUICK RELEASE.

Now, this does not mean drugs or partying. Tried that already (see e.g. drinking the entire bottle of wine, instead of a glass). This means try quick, simple pleasures to allow you to escape from reality, if only for a few minutes. Go shopping. Call a friend. Drink (a glass of) wine. This moment is not a permanent fix, nor is it meant to be. It's meant to relieve some immediate pressure while you compartmentalize your crap and figure out a real course of action.

CHAPTER 5: DESENSITIZED

Misery loves company.

I'M HUNGRY...I'M THIRSTY...I'M SCARED... I NEED A HUG...I NEED TO PEE

Bedtime. For the love of God. Bedtime.

My daughter is completely desensitized to any parenting either my husband or I give her at bedtime. Positive reinforcement. Negative reinforcement. No reinforcement. Nothing works. She still gets up, again and again.

We start the bedtime routine around 7:30 p.m. with a goal of bedtime around 8:00 p.m. Typically, our child will go to sleep after 9:00 p.m. What goes wrong? It's still a mystery we have not been able to solve.

Here's the bedtime routine:
1. Bath
2. Put on jammies
3. Brush teeth
4. Potty
5. Get blanket
6. Read books
7. Rub back

Step #7 happens an average of four to five times every night.

Okay. Positive reinforcement. We need a reward for staying in bed. I Pinterested a cute chart where you add stickers to get down the path and reach the castle. Once you reach the castle, you get ice cream. Piper loves ice cream. She loves stickers. This is a positive approach where there is a reward. Never worked. She couldn't connect the next morning getting a sticker or no sticker with whether she had stayed in bed the night before. If she hadn't stayed in bed, she just got very upset she didn't get a sticker. It created a new meltdown opportunity in the morning while trying to do the right thing.

Okay. Negative reinforcement. We'll take your blanket if you get up. This didn't really work either. All it did was prolong bedtime. When we took her blanket, she was definitely staying up until she got it back.

We tried putting her to bed later. We tried starting the bedtime process earlier. I even made up a song with all the bedtime actions beginning with a "B."

Bath, bajammies, brush, bathroom, blanket, books, and a back rub. Boodle be boo ba boo.

Nothing worked. She was going to go to bed when she wanted to.

Excuses rained down on us every night, and that's all they were... excuses. I'm hungry. I'm thirsty. I need to potty again. I need one more hug. I forgot to give the dog a hug. I saw a light out my window and got scared. I heard a noise and got scared again. You all didn't come and rub my back (for the 8th time) so I thought you left. I need a cracker. And a million more excuses. You fill in the blanks.

Every night, my husband and I think we've got her down. Ah, success.

Then, a little blond streak of hair will appear by the door. Then, we'll see a face and a child sucking her blanket (yeah, it's gross) and a grin. "Don't be mad, I just wanted to say I love you one more time." Dammit. What do you do with that? It's clearly an excuse, but one where you can't get mad at her.

My child is desensitized to my parenting at age three. I'm in trouble.

So is society.

Another great example of our ever-expanding desensitization and our need for the extreme is evident in comparing the TV shows *The West Wing* and *House of Cards*. The titles alone depict society's need for extra stimulation. The West Wing in the White House, which holds the oval office, used to be the most revered space in our country. The show, in its prime in the early 2000s, was intellectual. It was a positive storyline, always working toward doing good for the country and its people. *House of Cards* is over a decade later, and we all know what happens to a house made of cards. It falls. The show was about manipulation, murder, and selfish gain, the complete opposite of *The West Wing*. Granted, we cannot accurately extrapolate these fictional shows with today's politics or politicians. My point is, we crave the extreme to keep our attention because we have so much coming at us.

Desensitization is a result of needing to "check out" from reality. We've become so overstimulated with social media and instant access to any information we could possibly want that it takes the "extreme" to hold our attention. We've become a society with ADHD tendencies, creating a constant need for stimulation. "Checking out" has become our coping mechanism to deal with the chaos of life. How do we become re-engaged instead of disengaged?

What will be next? What will it take for us to be engaged in twenty years? A book used to do it. Social media now does it. What is next?

Couldn't we all use just a little more sleep?

Misery lo~~ves~~ company.

Misery loves those who
zone out.

CHALLENGE: ADD WORTH.

Mamas want to add worth to our children's lives. Well, we can't add worth if we are zoned out by the amount we have to get done.

In general, are you adding to or taking away from people's day? Do you lift others up or bring them down? Do you inspire or criticize? At some point, you have done all of the above. So think, what is your tendency?

It needs to be adding. Think about how you want to be treated. We are desensitized so much because we're battling fake all the time. Do we even know what we want, or are we becoming a zombie to survive?

Permission granted to go add worth to yourself. Once you do, it's much easier to add worth to others. Go do something that makes you feel alive.

Permission granted to give these a try...

1. TAKE A RISK

Otherwise, it is not satisfying because you didn't push any boundary. It was easy. Easy moves us toward depression. We are thankful that everyday things are easy for us, even Staples' marketing is the red "easy button." Easy doesn't help us. Easy keeps us from learning. Easy keeps us from toughing it out and making something of a bad situation. We all want easy. Yet, we all need a little more than easy.

You need to have the confidence to push yourself to do more. It's so easy to let the world spin by while you only get done what absolutely must get done.

Restructure your life to be able to take risks - fun ones (rock climbing), silly ones (playing on the playground *with* your kids instead of watching them), big ones (career move - if you're unhappy, it's worth it), and everyday ones (leaning in - thank you Sheryl Sandberg).

Sometimes I force myself to set a deadline just to get it done. I just put it out there so now I have to do it. Then, if I tell someone else my deadline, it motivates me get it done because I don't want to disappoint them.

When you have company visiting your house, you clean more. You complete tasks throughout your day because you can't risk someone thinking poorly of you. You have to get over the hump to make a task a risk for yourself. It doesn't have to be skydiving. It could be volunteering at a local nonprofit - refer to Chapter 2 about creating space in your day before you roll your eyes! Permission granted to break through the minutia and GO BIG.

2. APPRECIATE THE ANTICIPATION.

Think about Netflix. We've created a new phrase for it - "binge watching." We can no longer accept cable and its weekly schedule for our favorite shows. We would rather delay starting the first season and wait for it to come out on Netflix so we don't have to wait episode to episode, not to mention no commercials! We can access things so easily it doesn't provide the same feeling it used to.

A couple of decades ago, we physically had to walk into a library to complete a paper. Even though we didn't like it, we found satisfaction in the work to complete it. Now you don't have to work for it. You don't even have to leave your phone to communicate, shop, work, play games, or watch TV. Not only can you do all of those things on one device, you can do them all by yourself. No human interaction required.

3. Feel Something

Take a hike. Get sore. The physical part is easier. When it comes to emotions, they are much harder to navigate. We try to hide our emotions quite a bit. We don't want to cry at movies. We don't want to get overly excited in a meeting. We fight our emotions all the time. We consider that being strong. When used effectively, emotions are powerful tools that help us navigate and improve our world.

Or then again, you could be the exact opposite and feel too much. You can't keep it together because you're too emotional. For more on emotions, I challenge you to get to Chapter 8.

You decide how you handle your life. This action item is intended for those who feel like life has passed them by because they are too tired, too sad, or too late to do anything about it.

CHAPTER 6: GRUMPY

You are who you are.

I AM NOT WONDER WOMAN – I AM ME

Here's another "Mama Fail" for you. I asked Piper what she wanted to be for Halloween in September. Dumb. All I did was give her ample time to change her mind, a bunch of times. I proceeded to purchase Wonder Woman, Moana, Tinkerbell, and vampire costumes. Yes, I enabled this fail. She ended up going as a vampire for Halloween because, as she expressed, the others are more like everyday outfits. A vampire is definitely only for Halloween. Such is the rationale of a three-year-old.

From mid-September to Halloween, she wore Wonder Woman essentially everywhere except school. I made up a policy that the costume wasn't allowed at daycare, and thankfully she bought it.

One day, I'm at the store with Piper. She's all decked out in her Wonder Woman costume, and a very nice, well-intentioned lady said, "Oh wow, there's Wonder Woman." It made Piper grumpy. She quickly responded, "I am NOT Wonder Woman. I am Piper," and gave a reassuring nod to this lady. In this moment, it was cute. If this continues beyond her toddler years, this scenario is no longer cute. In fact, if this behavior lingers, you have the lady walking away saying, "What a brat," under her breath.

For now, let's be relieved she knows herself and likes herself and thinks others should, too. She wants to be Piper. That's good enough for me. Most kids have more confidence than adults because they don't yet have life experiences to make them cynical, insecure, and hopeless. Unfortunately, kids eventually get there. Adults have had plenty of time for grumpy to settle in.

Piper continued the Halloween season getting grumpy in public when people said she was Wonder Woman. She was angry, because she wanted to be *her*. We are angry because we're not someone *else*. What's wrong with us? Let's start telling the world, I AM MAMA!

Why do we allow negativity to bring us down?

You are ~~who~~ you are.

Normal is the new awesome.

CHALLENGE: FIGHT GRUMPY.

Piper was grumpy for the right reason. She wanted people to know she was Piper, NOT Wonder Woman. We strive every day to be some better version of someone else (or worse, the unrealistic, unattainable Wonder Woman). Stop fighting. Stop being grumpy at yourself. Be good to yourself.

Here's a scenario for you: Which person do you think walked away having a better day?

Scenario 1: Gertrude
Car won't start. Missed breakfast. Late to meeting, so the team didn't use my idea. Mom called and ranted about me not visiting enough. Realized I missed a deadline. Scrolled through Facebook and noticed everyone is having a better day than me. Come home. No food in fridge. Kid is hangry. Boss calls while kid is wailing in the background. Power goes out, and I just realize I am out of Xanax.

Scenario 2: Grace
A neighbor helped me out at 6:30 in the morning. Was being so productive I looked up, and it was lunch time. I rushed to a meeting and learned I needed to get to know this group better. Taking a break, I realized Facebook has a lot of people who need love and support. Take out night! Let kids go play outside while I take a quick call from the boss. Power goes out - found the candles and told scary stories under the covers. Didn't even need my pills. Too tired to notice.

Insert your day here. We choose how we define our day.

Which day do you want? You'll take the second one every time. Why do you tend to relay your day in the voice of the first example? We can't help it. It's nature.

Permission granted to find grace for yourself. Grumpy never made anyone feel better, even if you know people who wear it well.

Permission granted to give these a try...

1. USE POSITIVE FIRST.

Positivity is not necessarily subconscious. Some people do it better than others. Working positive language into your life is good for you. It will make you feel better. It will make others feel better. It is an encouraging tone versus a defeated tone. Think back to examples where you wish your boss, husband, kid, etc. would have approached something more positively. What are you giving to others?

When is the right time to be negative? I would say it a different way... When to be honest and when to accept responsibility. I'm not trying to ignore difficult situations. I just think it's worth trying to frame hardships with some glimmer of hope through positive words.

Let's try to be a little more positive. Here are some samples as you write emails, send texts, respond to posts, or have a conversation with someone.

Negative
My daughter left her terrible twos only to become a raging threenager.

Positive
My spirited daughter loves all things magical and has found a sense of independence all on her own.

Negative
Hate to miss it.

Positive
Wish I could come.

Negative
Let's not dwell on the past.

Positive
Let's focus on the future.

Negative
You have a problem with people. You don't work on your deficiency. You clearly don't get along with others.

Positive
I see a lot of potential with you when it comes to people. Let's try to find some ways to improve your relationships because you have a lot to offer others.

You're the only one who can determine whether or not you're happy. Decide to do it. Use positive language in your life. It will affect everyone around you, including yourself.

2) SMILE.

Smiling is simple, yet not natural. RBF was coined for a reason. Our resting face does not necessarily translate to our mood or temperament. Be aware of your face as people talk to you. The most common misperception is intently listening. You think that's awesome. They think you're a bitch.

Here's a good way to gauge your face. What are you doing while you drive? Think about it. It's likely not smiling.

Smiling comes natural to me. I like to make people happy. Smiling is one of the easiest ways to do that. However, I still have RBF sometimes. I can't help it. I don't even know I'm doing it!

I'm sure everyone has heard that it takes more muscles to frown than to smile. While that's true, it takes essentially no muscles to pull off RBF.

Try to smile at fifteen people per day. This might seem like a lot to someone who isn't used to smiling. That's why it's a challenge. Think of it this way - It's less than one person per your awake hours (unless you're the fortunate mama getting 9+ hours of sleep). You can be walking by them, across the room in a meeting, in front of them at the grocery store checkout, or getting ready to ask them something.

Now for those of you who still have no ideas what RBF is... Resting Bitch Face. Ah, now it all makes sense...

For those of you who don't smile, you definitely think this is stupid. I get it. This crazy lady says we should smile more often and success will come. Well, it's one of the first steps to liking yourself better, and maybe brightening someone else's day. Think about how much a smile would mean coming from someone who doesn't smile all that much. What's so wrong with that?

Smiling is free. Smiling is simple. Dieting is hard. Dieting makes me sad. I choose smiling. What an unfair comparison - yep, it is.

3. WATCH YOUR MICRO EXPRESSIONS.

Nonverbal communication is what we see when we're not talking, and often, it speaks the loudest. Micro expressions are those tiny little flinches, good or bad, your body does when you react to something. Someone asks a stupid question. You likely give a micro expression with your eyes, reflecting you thought that was a stupid question.

When someone says something really nice to you, you have the opposite reaction. Your eyes brighten. People pick up on these micro expressions, too, and they affect your relationships deeply.

Be conscious of the messages you're sending out into the world.

Part III:
What's Happening to Me?

CHAPTER 7: CIVILITY
Two wrongs don't make a right.

I Don't Love You Right Now

"Mama, I don't love you right now. I only love Daddy." Screaming, "Mama, no! Don't touch me. I only want Daddy!"

Daddy jumps in and says, "Now, we do not talk to your mama like that. That is not acceptable behavior. Say you're sorry."

"I'm sorry, mama. I just don't like you right now, okay?"

These periods can go on for minutes or days. Sometimes, thankfully, I'm on the receiving end of love, and Daddy gets the cold shoulder.

My daughter is just developing boundaries. She's taking risks to learn how to navigate emotions and what they mean. No big deal. She has an excuse. Adults do not.

It's easy to be mean. It's much harder to overlook your thoughts, assumptions, and sometimes, beliefs, to be nice. Much harder.

For example, high school is hard. Drama swarms around you, and it's easy to get sucked in. I've noticed those who say they have no drama tend to be in the center of the cyclone.

I was busy in high school. I was in the marching band with rehearsals on Monday and Thursday and ball games on Friday. I played tennis during the week and had matches before band rehearsal nights. I danced and sprinkled in rehearsals and performances where I could.

I do not say this to brag. I say this to share how little time I had to develop relationships, and it showed. When I worried about not having friends, adults said it was jealousy. I said it was mean. It was probably both.

It was Halloween night of my junior year. I wasn't dressing up. I was going to give out candy with my Papaw. Cute characters started coming to the door as soon as dusk fell. Batman, She-Ra (my favorite), Mickey Mouse, Disney princesses, and cute baby ladybugs and pumpkins whose parents eat all their candy.

And then, *they* showed up, my "friends."

They came to my door and said, "Trick or treat," and I gave them candy. My heart sank. I not only didn't get invited to go trick or treating, but they had the audacity to show up and make it *known* I was not invited. My Papaw noticed it bothered me, and said, "Ah, don't worry about them. You were nice to give them candy. You're a good girl."

While my encounter was face-to-face, a majority of bullying (it's a strong word for my experience, but the point remains true) takes place on a social landscape. Social media runs rampant with insulated regurgitated words. What I mean is Facebook algorithms give you what you want to see.[8] You see more of what you like and share, so it insulates your beliefs because you only see what you believe. Unless you're actively searching for the other side of the story, you will not get it in your news feed. People feel left out. People feel alone. And quite often, people remain the silent majority.

Therefore, I have developed a different definition for the word opinion. How can it be an opinion if you didn't have a fair amount of knowledge to form the idea? Rarely do we seek reputable sources and review opposing sides to formulate our own opinion about something. Our brain can only absorb so much at one time, so it's easy to take your friend's well-written Facebook post and accept it as truth. These are regurgitated words, not an educated opinion.

I'll step off my proverbial soapbox now and get back to my sad misery of being a loner in high school. Today, these mean behaviors don't take place on the playground and in person. They take place on a much bigger stage for the world to see. We hide behind posts and say mean things we wouldn't say to someone's face. It's easy because patronizing or demeaning posts often do not see a consequence.

So, for all those who felt left out, embarrassed, or bullied, don't be them. Be better.

Better is hard. Mean is easy.

Two wrongs do~~n~~Xt make a right.

If you keep going right, you'll come full circle.

CHALLENGE: RISE ABOVE.

It's so easy to be a part of the negative. It's pretty much human nature. How often do you think you rise above versus lower yourself? When I think of rising above, I think of something that always does this and doesn't even realize it.

A dog.

Think about the unconditional love a dog has for its owner. We should try and be more like dogs. When there is nothing nice to say, a dog says nothing at all. When you've left them all day alone in the house, they are still excited to see you. Their sweet eyes never give a mean look. Yes, we should definitely try to be more like dogs.

Until we can understand the love a dog shares, we will not move beyond tolerance to love. We must find a way to love people, no matter what, so our future can lay the groundwork for meaningful change. We must pause. We must give space. We must find empathy for all and be better.

While Piper is still learning, and my "friends" were immature, adults don't have an excuse. We must rise above to be better examples for our children. They are paying attention.

Permission granted to give these a try...

1. LEARN THE LESSON.

Bad experiences can teach you what you don't want to be - sometimes a harsh form of awareness, yet it builds resilience. We need more of that.

I once had a boss who told me to my face I was incompetent after I had just landed a huge deal. It made no sense. I had just made the boss look good. This person should be happy, but they were not. Over time, it became a hostile working environment that was affecting me physically and emotionally. We just didn't mix. The day I walked away from that situation was the day I told myself to reframe my experience. The boss can now be viewed as just a person, no longer a demeaning boss. Period. I walked away without baggage. I walked away with knowledge, provided by a bad boss, of what I never, ever want to be for anybody else. Lesson learned.

While guided by stress, frustration, and hurt, I'm glad I had this negative experience. You don't grow when you're content with your life. You miss so much when you're just hanging out in a solid, good environment. Very little learning happens until you're pushed.

Push yourself to learn the lesson.

2. UNDERSTAND YOUR LANDSCAPE.

I've worked in the communications field, and I'm convinced only 10% are engaged and informed and know what's going on. I think another 10% are just mad all the time, like to argue, and can't figure out why they are frustrated. These are our loud voices. Everything is black and white. There is no gray. The squeaky wheel gets the oil and the ratings, so it's easy to be skewed on what everyone thinks, and that's just 20% of people.

What are the other 80% doing?

Surviving life is what they are doing! They don't have time for any wasted space, so things that don't affect them, don't get noticed.

Why are we so easily frustrated by the mad 10%? It's human nature. If 80% of people are not paying attention, why are you focusing so much time on the 10% who don't agree with you? You have to trust your gut and move on. Don't get hung up on my gut feeling about percentages. Just know it's hard to deal and easy to be misled by a loud voice.

Rise above and work to be the 10% who are engaged and informed and making peace in their own world, both professionally, personally, and publicly!

3. BE MORE LIKE A DOG

Dogs have unconditional love. They always forgive and are always by your side with a wagging tail. Man's best friend didn't come out of the blue; it's real.

My current boss is a dog, and I mean that in the best way possible. I have the best boss. His ability to deal with ignorance is fascinating. On Myers-Briggs, he's in the minority as a male with a high F for feeling. Yet, he controls his emotions beautifully. He gets dealt crap daily and always rises above. He absorbs all the pain from everyone and only projects love to others. Inside, I'm sure he has days he doubts, worries, or maybe even spews. It never shows. The golden rule is his mantra. It's why so many people think they can dump on him because he can handle it. Is it fair? No. Do they realize how they sound when they complain? No. It's because he rises above with everyone he encounters. My boss is a dog. We should all try to be more like my boss.

CHAPTER 8: AWARENESS

Hindsight is 20/20.

Mama, Why is She So Fat

We all have moments when our children embarrass us. Here's one of mine.

I'm picking up Piper from school one day, and like normal, we have a routine of things we must do prior to actually leaving. Visit the babies. Hug best friends. Check locker for new pictures. And the infamous, "Mama, I'm not done playing yet." See, she really does like going to school once she puts on her clothes!

I said, "Piper, let's go! I have to go to the grocery store and be home in thirty minutes. Can you help me with that?" She just looks at me and says, "No. I wanna stay here." The teacher had to help us get out the door. Yep, she's still desensitized to my parenting.

At the grocery store, she's running up and down the aisles, touching everything. I finally get the three items I need, and we make our way to the checkout. All of a sudden, Piper turns around and asks, "Mama, why is she so fat?"

There's a lady behind me, and she hears Piper. Uh oh, I'm 99% sure she is the person Piper is referring to.

My face starts blotching instantly, heart racing. What in the hell do I do to fix this moment? Oh my.

First, I react and say, "Piper, that's not nice!" Then, I look at the lady and beg for an apology via my sad face. Well, that doesn't work because Piper proceeds to then say, "But mama, she's really big, right?"

Sweat beads start forming on my forehead. I can feel them. I then proceed to act like Piper didn't say anything, because I am so mortified that I draw a blank on how to handle this. I turn around quickly only to knock down the point-of-sale suckers, and they crash to the ground. Of course, they are the big round ones that roll all around the floor and even under this lady's shopping cart.

Oh dear. I tear up and just start saying "I'm sorry," over and over to no one in particular. Piper is standing there shocked and now wants a sucker. I just give her a firm look and say, "Help me pick these up. Now!"

"Okay, mama. I'm sorry I said that."

The lady leans over and starts picking up some suckers. Now I feel even worse. She walks over to me like she's going to say something. My heart starts racing even faster. I'm not ready, not prepared for this conversation.

The lady says, "Dear. She's just little. It's okay. Plus, I know I'm fat," and she smiles and lets out a little laugh.

What just happened? She rose above, and I'm still hanging out in failure mode and can't deal with life.

In that moment, Piper lacked awareness. She had no clue her question had the potential to hurt someone's feelings. In her mind, she was just stating the obvious. This innocence is many times categorized as cute or sweet. It's only those few, raw exceptions where you want to go crawl in a hole for that sweet (and completely embarrassing) innocent kiddo who will say whatever is on her mind.

As adults, we say and do things daily that offend, hurt, distract, and frustrate. The likelihood that we truly know it - null, nada, nope. We're oblivious.

We are sometimes the recipients of these actions. Why in the world would we not think we are also thoughtless participants, too? We don't, though. We just don't.

Ian Cron, best-selling author who spoke at Leadercast 2018, stated that only 13% of all people are truly self-aware.[4] What? Not possible. You know what that means? You got it... **87% of people THINK they are self-aware**.

Do you have a micromanager for a boss? In their mind, they just want to make sure they achieve excellence. Got a helicopter parent? They just want to ensure the best for you. Have a lazy friend? Maybe they only relax with a true friend, which they consider you to be.

See... these scenarios barely scratch the surface of what happens in our daily lives and in the multitude of interactions that have the potential of mistaken intent.

Hindsight ~~is~~ X 20/20.

foresight is foggy.

CHALLENGE: ADOPT ADAPTING.

We are so focused on our own needs and how to survive life, we often forget other people have needs, too. We don't understand why someone frustrates us or why someone is so difficult to work with. Have you ever thought that it could be you? Likely not. Unless you have a life coach, you probably have never considered YOU are the problem.

If you could remove a frustration from your life, would you do it? Of course, you would! So why don't you? Well, that means YOU would have to adjust your thoughts, feelings, or actions. Frankly, we won't do it. It's almost like we can't, like we're hardwired to accept only what we were taught to believe, even when given overwhelming evidence contradicting our beliefs.

It's amazing to watch. We're so rigid, have such a need for control, yet we struggle to understand why we don't perform better in teams. The give and take is missing because we live under the false assumption that everyone *else* needs to give a little. Why? Because I'm right, *right*?

In order to be more aware, we must be adaptable. No more "it's all about me" mentality. Once you become more aware, you'll notice other people's tendencies, and then you can adapt to improve your relationships. While compromise seems like a bad word in politics, it's a healthy word for relationships.

Permission granted to give these a try...

1. KNOW YOUR AUDIENCE.

If you don't know yourself, how in the world can you expect to know your audience? Knowing your audience, believe it or not, is much easier. You do it all the time. You judge.

Now, it's about learning how to effectively assess versus judge.

I'm a fan of the *Personality Style at Work* Assessment.[5] *Personality Style at Work* is an assessment used to improve effectiveness of communications and to influence others. The assessment allows you to become more self-aware regarding your own reactions and tendencies. It also helps you diagnose others' personalities in an effort to adapt to your environment and increase productivity. Essentially, it provides a roadmap that allows you to remove frustrations in your life. Who doesn't want that? In fact, it has a supplemental book called *How to Work with (Almost) Anyone*.[6] See, that should make you feel better. Some people can't be helped, even the experts agree. That isn't you or you wouldn't have read this far.

The four core personalities are Direct, Spirited, Systematic, and Considerate. It's actually straightforward and relatively easy to diagnose if you know what you're looking for.

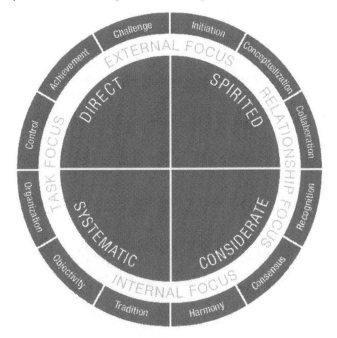

I'm a Spirited. I know this. I've taken a (ridiculous) number of assessments because I want to understand my tendencies as well as my frustrations.

Spirited people are cheerleaders, the ultimate motivators. They get people excited about a cause, a mission, a project, or a mama simply working in a nap. They are notorious for making people feel special. That all sounds fabulous, doesn't it?

Guess what else Spiriteds do?

We overwhelm. We instantly love an idea without any knowledge of its ability to actually work (and we can convince you it's brilliant when there are a million holes). We talk a lot. We can be loud. We love to exaggerate. Basically, we have the ability to wear people out and leave them figuring out how to avoid us.

We all have good and bad traits. We all have strengths and weaknesses. The most critical point is to understand good and bad, and make sure your thoughts match reality. I try and make people happy by hugging and smiling and telling a story to make them laugh. That works for some people. For others, I exaggerate and am too much for people. How do you know how to be?

You must temper and intensify.

It's not about you. Would you be willing to adapt your behavior in an effort to better work in a team setting (or family setting)? Most people would be willing to give that a try, right? Why is it that Uncle Bob always gets on our nerves, and we're terrible at hiding it? We are not thinking about him. We're only concerned with our own feelings.

Basically, we're selfish. We just are, and we can't help it. Therefore, we must fight it.

2. BE LIKABLE.

Why in the world are you not? If you're not, you likely don't find value in it. Being tough is more important. It shows you're serious, and you mean business. Well, if someone in your world needs encouragement, then your tough attitude will eventually make them leave, and in the present, will definitely make them talk badly about you behind your back.

Did you know 75% of employees leave bosses not companies?[7]
That is close to the number of people who are not self-aware.

Hmmm... Any correlation? I bet it's a strong one!

Being likable is half the battle. If you're likable, people want to help you. If you are likable, people are willing to listen to you. If you are likable, sometimes you get the job not based on merit but because you are more pleasant to work with.

Improving your emotional intelligence allows you to be more likable. You've adjusted to the emotional needs of others to accomplish a goal. It's THE key to improving relationships. It's a real skill. It comes more natural to some, but in the end, it can and must be learned. If nothing else, you will just feel better at life if you're aware of who you are and who you're around. Essentially, emotional intelligence is a critical 21st-century skill.

3. PAUSE.

Reactions can be hard to overcome. Even if it seems like an awkward pause, trust me, that's better than flies swarming out of your mouth like John Coffey in *The Green Mile*. Can't really take it back.

When you were in school, did you take a math exam without checking any of your answers? No. Do you spit out a reply to your boss and immediately push send? I'm guessing not. Do you react to your kid doing something wrong? Well, probably. (Forget that last one.)

Typically, you take a second to make sure the action is right. So, let's start doing that before we speak. An immediate response is not required.

Pause before you blunder.

CHAPTER 9: FILTER

Don't judge a book by its cover.

Your Sinus Infection Makes Me Want to Punch You

It has been said when you have lemons, make lemonade. Try this one. When life throws you rotten lemons, you deal, right? Then, someone thinks they have rotten lemons too, when they actually just have perfectly fine lemons. Why are they so upset? We know how to freakin' deal with just normal lemons. We do that ALL the time. (Insert eye roll.)

Why do we get frustrated? It's because we filter others. Others filter us. Most often, without all the details, we make assumptions based on our current state of mind, not necessarily the facts or details.

Think about cool, Instagram filters. The intent is to make something seem slightly different, and in most cases, better than it is. We don't think the real photo is good enough, so we feel the need to improve it.

The opposite is also true. Sometimes, we don't improve. Sometimes, we filter by leaving out. We *don't* share a story, or we limit details, because we don't want people to know what's really going on.

You never know what someone else is going through. That's likely because they are not telling you. For example, mamas don't want pity. They want to seem like they can handle it.

On the other hand, people may embellish what they're going through so you'll notice, so you'll pay a little extra attention. How many of you have read a cryptic Facebook post from a "friend" who won't share what's wrong, and deep down they are just dying for you to ask? They need attention. Or they really need someone to understand.

We all filter in our own way.

Are your filters realistic, fake, positive, negative, nonexistent, or something else?

Going back to my crazy few weeks of family emergencies, guess what I left out? I had a sinus infection. One day, I was zoning out on social media, and I ran across this post:

I really hate to post this, and I never do things like this, but I wanted to let you know that if I'm not my bubbly self today, I apologize in advance. I have the absolute worst sinus infection in the world. It's really got me down. I feel awful.

Her sinus infection made me want to punch her.

I had a freakin' sinus infection too, and it felt like a paper cut based on what everyone else in my family was dealing with. Just so you know, I only punched her in the face in my mind. It felt good.

Then, I wondered if she was filtering. Probably so.

People filter all the time. What I should have done was rise above and let her have her moment. Maybe the sinus infection was the only thing she was willing to post at that time. Maybe she just needed someone to understand she was having a hard time. Maybe she needed someone to say it was okay. Maybe her sinus infection was the last straw in her life, her "fruit and cheese."

We all have stories. It's *how* we choose to tell them... or *if* we choose to tell them. We share a story in different ways simply because of who we're telling. Good, bad, sad, or indifferent - the story told, depends on the situation at hand and the audience before you. Here's a classic example. Teenager tells mom she's going to a friend's house. Teenager tells friends she's going to a hip party. We all filter.

Every day, you decide which version you will let the world in on. Most people with traumatic experiences do not share the gory details. Many times, people have no idea what others are going through, and that's okay. Mamas don't want to be whiners. We don't want to show weakness. We filter to be strong.

We all have crazy, dysfunctional family and friend moments, and in time, we choose whether or not we are fine. Some people have had seriously traumatic moments that are unbearable. Some people have had bad days that linger. All experiences are relative, depending on your filter.

Bad moments are just as defining as shining moments. I would argue a few bad moments are required for growth and development.

What are your short-term (sinus infection) and long-term (family) filters? What slant are you putting on your life? Are you filtering a symptom or a root cause? Is it superficial or deep-rooted?

Be sensitive to what people are and (more importantly) aren't telling you.

Be able to find that filter.

Don't judge ~~a book by its cover.~~

Judge a book around
Chapter 3.

CHALLENGE: FIND YOUR FILTER

Just like you filter a story depending on who you're telling, expect others to be doing that to you, too. Filters are sometimes necessary, sometimes not. Filters sometimes improve a story, and sometimes they exaggerate it to the point of ridiculousness. Sometimes we leave out too much information and it's confusing.

What's your filter? Is it different for different people? It should be. Otherwise, you're likely unaware of the effect your words have on others. If you're not appropriately filtering, you're not making an attempt to filter (adapt to) your audience.

Permission granted to give these a try...

1. APPRECIATE FRUSTRATIONS.

Sounds ridiculous, ay? A frustration typically starts because someone has filtered or not filtered something.

When you have a frustration, you have to figure out how to handle it. Often times, we are passive aggressive and hold in our anger. We need to accept that we are frustrated and then work to fix it. When you fix it, you feel good about it. When you don't, you bottle emotions over and over, and then spew on somebody about something insignificant! Then, you're embarrassed and now you're viewed as crazy. It happened to me! I had been filtering to everyone outside my family because I needed to be strong. There was no time to let my guard down. There was no time to get upset. I just had to do life (with no fruit and cheese).

You learn more about how to be better the next time around when you appreciate frustrations. While it may be a little annoying in the process, you're better for it. It's like satisfaction - it's not quite as fleeting if you had to overcome a few bumps along the way. If you can appreciate frustrations, the end result is more rewarding. If it's all easy, you likely didn't appreciate anything.

2. GIVE THEM ONE ROUND.

You don't know how many layers you aren't hearing from someone by the time they get to you. Think about all the things you aren't sharing with someone. If it's eating at you, it's likely noticeable, but people don't know why. Wouldn't you hope someone would give you the benefit of the doubt and let something go if you were having a hard time?

We try every day to act like we have it all together. We protect our weaknesses by putting on a good face. We do it for our family. We do it for our boss and colleagues. When do we ever let our guard down? Never. Because somehow, it always comes back to haunt us. So, since you're hell-bent on acting like you've got it all "handled" (sure do miss Olivia Pope), you better try and deal with your stress in a manageable, bite-sized way.

We play different roles. They change daily depending on what we're celebrating or tackling.

Work to peel back the layers of someone before you make a determination regarding their character, true abilities, or current state of stress.

3. Stop talking

Like you were told when you were young, "If you don't have something nice to say, don't say anything at all." Just be quiet. This is so easy to say, and much harder to do. Start counting to ten in your head during frustrating encounters with kids or adults. Don't say *anything* for at least ten seconds. This allows you to pause, reframe the situation, and possibly avoid getting worked up in the first place!

PART IV:
I CAN DO THIS

CHAPTER 10: CHARACTER

Actions speak louder than words.

Mud Makes it Better

My Papaw is part of the Greatest Generation. I witnessed character and honor displayed at home as I was growing up. It's something I value and yearn to teach Piper. My hope for this world is that Piper's generation will be the next greatest generation. I believe this. We have to start now to make sure that happens.

My Papaw is 85 years old and has neuropathy in his legs. Therefore, he can't feel from his knees down. He also suffered a couple of back-to-back mini strokes, but he never let me go to the doctor with him. He said he had it covered. After his second mini stroke, I made an effort to find out when his neurology appointment was scheduled. It took some sneakiness, but nonetheless, I was going.

The day of the appointment, Papaw walks into the waiting area with a basket of fresh vegetables. This is Papaw. Always doing something special for someone else.

They call his name, and we go back to see the neurologist. When the doctor comes in, he sees the vegetables and says, "Well, that's some good-looking vegetables there. Where did you get those?"

Without skipping a beat, Papaw says, "I picked them fresh from my garden. I know how you like tomatoes."

The doctor looks puzzled, "You mean someone picked them from a garden for you?"

"No sir," Papaw says, "I still tend to a garden. These are from my garden out at the farm." Papaw goes on to talk about "kids these days" and how they are not trying hard enough because they don't understand the value of work like his generation does.

The doctor asks, "Well, how do you do it?"

Papaw laughs saying, "I crawl, doc. Nothing stopping me from crawling! In fact, I like it best after it's rained a bit. Once the knees on my pants get muddy, they kinda act like knee pads. Mud makes it better. Works real nice."

The doctor just shakes his head with a smile and says, "Well then. Thank you very much for the vegetables from *your* garden."

That's a special story about my Papaw. It says so much about him. He never complains, and despite his condition and age, his work ethic has never faltered. He demands so much of himself and expects nothing from others. He has character. He's working so hard at age 85 to remain engaged in life, to remain relevant.

Are we, no matter our age, working to be good people, doing good things?

People talk about altruism. Even when people are trying their best to be altruistic, I believe there is still a tiny portion of self-serving that drives the act. Not my Papaw. For him, true joy is seeing others happy. That's all he needs.

I want to be like that. Just like that.

What is it that makes someone good? It's not that simple; it's rather complex.

My Papaw had many moments in his life as a Depression baby that required him to garner resilience. He never wanted anyone else to feel like he did or experience poverty like he had.

My Nanny and Papaw raised me. Let's just say, I survived a few things between ages six and eight. Yep - I'm filtering! Living with my grandparents was the best thing that could have happened to me.

I am who I am today because of the many unintentional lessons my grandparents taught me. My Papaw knew how to tell a good story and make people feel special. My Nanny knew how to give. When you combine the two, I learned how to make people feel special through my words and my actions.

These are all qualities I hope Piper possesses one day. I also hope Piper tends to a garden, just like her Great-Papaw, and refuses to stop.

Actions Speak Louder
Than Words.

Revealing good is the loudest
sound of all.

CHALLENGE: STRETCH YOUR RELEVANCE.

Why do you think it's important to stretch before and after you exercise? To warm up and cool down your muscles. Stretching the muscles keeps them healthy and strong. So, why then, do we not work to stretch our mind, thus stretching our relevance?

How hard are you working to be relevant? Are you content with where you are? Is that a good or bad thing? Are you a role model for your children? Are you pushing yourself or whining about being busy?

Stretch goals exist in businesses and nonprofits. Do they exist in your life? It's like reaching for the moon and landing on a star. Are you just getting by, or are you working to be relevant in your world? Going the extra mile? Learning because you enjoy it? Adding in more kiddo time versus work time? How are you stretching?

People want to leave a legacy. They want to remain relevant as long as they live. Mamas - let's not wait until the end of our lives to start. Let's start now.

Permission granted to give these a try...

1. REFLECT ON WHAT MATTERS.

We spend so much energy either about things we cannot control or things that won't matter in a week. It's wasted space that could have been used for good. When you reflect on what matters, your path forward is stronger.

How do you define what matters? Here's a quick test:

- Try and recall the last five Golden Globe winners (without Googling it).

  You may get one or two if you're lucky.

- Now, try and think about five people who have helped you do something.

  That list is much easier.

Why is the second list so much easier? It's because those people are real to you. They did something specifically for you. They were relevant. Be personal and be memorable.

2. FIND JOY IN THE LITTLE THINGS.

I ran across a picture of a crowd at a concert. The first row was up against a fence. Of the 100+ people in the photo, only one of them did not have a phone out taking a picture of what was going on. Hey - I'm all about documenting your life for memories. This photo just spoke to me because of the lady's face; she simply had her arms on the fence, smiling. She was taking in the moment, enjoying it immensely. Everyone else seemed to be trying to capture the moment so they could tell others about it. She found joy in a small thing others couldn't find.

A small budding flower on the sidewalk. A nice breeze on a warm day. A kid saying thank you without prompt. The small things working in life lead to big things that matter. Appreciate those small things.

3. Be a little stubborn if it's important.

Let me clarify. This does not mean be rude, disrespectful, curt, or a martyr. Hold firm when it matters. I have a good friend who shared a story about her kid wanting a toy in a store. The kid was told he was not getting a toy. Temper tantrum ensued. Most mamas, after 20 minutes of wailing, would have given in and offered a toy to get him to stop crying and embarrassing her, but not this mom. She walked up and down aisles for over an hour (which she didn't have) telling her child they will not leave with a toy, and they will not leave until he pulled it together. Guess what? He eventually stopped crying, and he never did that again.

If we can hold firm when it matters, even if it takes longer, it's worth it.

CHAPTER 11: BALANCE

The grass is always greener on the other side.

EXTREME GOOD COMES FROM BALANCE

Technology is accelerating at such a frantic pace that you can customize almost anything for yourself. Want custom Oakley glasses? Check. Want a custom Coach purse? Check. Custom clothes for your children and family? Check. How in the world do we keep up? How in the world do we figure out what matters? It's easy to feel defeated when it appears everyone has more than you do. I'm almost convinced the more perfect a Facebook feed looks, the more "stuff" going on behind the scenes. Some serious filtering going on!

You know how the side mirrors on your car say, "Objects in mirror may be closer than they appear." The mirror of social media can also distort the truth. We believe other people's lives seem better than ours because they appear to be better. People are missing the meaning of life. The constant competition to post a better family photo is exhausting.

Let's take, for example, a couple of different approaches...

Materialists. (Let's suggest we are talking about baby boomers.) They worked their entire lives to acquire wealth, get more stuff. Bigger houses, bigger cars, and the membership to the country club are all on the list. Their parents had nothing, and by golly, they weren't going to let that happen to them.

Stuff. So much stuff. The feeling you get from obtaining the newest, best, and shiniest new something is all but a fleeting satisfaction that leaves us too quickly. We can't keep up. We end up wanting more and more, until we can no longer manage it. If you've ever moved, you know how much you accumulate. How much is meaningful? How much provided purpose?

Minimalists. (Let's suggest we are talking about millennials.) Is minimalism the new trendy thing? Actually, I hope a smidge of it is here to stay. Minimalists often do without things that don't provide purpose. They are downsizing their homes, taking bikes to work, and living greener in an effort to save the planet.

I think something between a minimalist and a materialist is a nice balance.

Let's call them Momentalists.

Momentalists. (Hopefully Piper's generation will evolve into this.) Momentalists understand the balance between experience and stuff. This balance comes from action that leads to purpose or achievement. They live in moments, and each moment is meant to be meaningful and have purpose. They hope, they love, they work hard, and they have respect. They are the best melding of all generations.

The opposite, however, is the deadliest yet. The worst of generations. The ones deprived of human interaction for the sake of technology advancement. Those who live connected to a device instead of people are off balance in another way. It's nice not to have to go to the grocery store and just pick up at the curb. It's nice to deposit a check with my phone. What worries me is the continued lack of human interaction we need to be socially adept at, I don't know, being good people!

We can still find balance. For example, having a nice car can be a valuable lesson if you're taught to take care of it.

We have to show value in being a momentalist. How to be real and how to be good.

My fear is Piper's generation will only know a hyper-customizing life. They will not need to know how to fix things, because if something breaks, they can replace it easier than fixing the original. They will encounter a problem, and a computer-generated solution will pop up for their specific problem. No need to surf YouTube for the video; it will be customized for them, their very own YouTube channel.

Thinking will no longer need to occur. Problem solving will be automated. How will this generation interact? They may not. They may live their day through virtual-reality goggles in an effort to be "connected."

I hope we can bring together the best traits of each generation in an effort to prepare our children for their future. Extreme good will come from the balance of being "all in" where it matters.

These life lessons are not unique. However, they may need to be uniquely applied to what our children will be facing.

The grass is a̶l̶w̶a̶y̶s̶ greener
on the o̶t̶h̶e̶r̶ side.

The grass is always greener
when you water it.

CHALLENGE: BE THE BUBBLE.

When you hang a picture on a wall, you use a leveler. Why? To make sure it's even. Same goes for installing a car seat. The bubble must be in the middle.

I struggle when people say they are too busy because they have a full plate. I roll my eyes and think to myself, "Upgrade your appetizer plate." This is my reaction. It may be yours. However, it goes against everything I'm asking you to do to reach your potential and be a great role model for your kids. Ugh. I still have to work on this one.

Still, people annoy me when they say they are "so busy." Stop talking about how busy you are and you would get more done! Sometimes, even my passive aggressiveness comes out and I say, "Oh, I can do that for you. I only have these 20 things to finish before I have to pick up my daughter at 5:30 p.m." See... we all have to work on balance at times.

Balance is the key to your attitude, emotions, and productivity. If you have balance, you can have peace with your priorities and relentlessly pursue them when it's time.

Permission granted to give these a try...

1. TAKE INVENTORY OF YOUR LIFE.

Mamas are usually moving so quickly, they never slow down to think through their life. Next time you're sitting in the school pick-up line (or any other moment you need a way to pass the time), start by building out buckets on paper, and adding items into them. Examples include family, work, volunteering, or you could look at daily versus weekly items.

Find where you need to add and where you need to take away. Then, reassess your priorities to make sure they are in line with what you want for yourself. If you don't know where to start, make four buckets for the four rooms as mentioned in Chapter 2.

2. CELEBRATE CULMINATING MOMENTS.

Enjoy the big stuff, and then realize it's the small stuff that gets you the big stuff. Let's take a wedding, for example. The big moment is actually getting married, but it is the thousands of decisions a bride made months in advance that will allow her to enjoy her day.

Kindergarten graduation. First day of school. Yeah... I check out for a couple of days on Facebook to avoid the onslaught of first-day-of-school photos. Are you taking time to really celebrate your kiddo's moment, or are you just thinking about your perfect post for social media?

First steps. Riding a bike. Every birthday. Getting a ribbon at the science fair. So many moments. These are all moments that are *big* to the kid and *super big* to the parents. Yet, oh-so-quickly posted and passed.

Celebrate BIG. Go all out. Why not? Those milestones build confidence and shape your kid. All the small stuff that got you there will likely be forgotten. Big moments are remembered. Then, those precious stories get passed down. Your social media feed will fade.

3. FIND GUILT-FREE PRIORITIES.

How many times have you felt guilty for working late or guilty for leaving early? How many times have you felt guilty for not spending enough time with your kids? How many times have you asked why only 24 hours exist in a day?

Set priorities that you (and your partner, if one is in the picture) deem appropriate. When you settle on what that is, you should not have guilt because you know your path. For example, I have to work late at least four nights per month. I make up that time by always taking Piper to school the next morning. It balances out, and there is no guilt. When Piper went to dance class in the afternoon, I would always check email and follow up on work items before bed. No need to feel guilty there. You have to understand your boundaries and be comfortable with the path forward. Feeling guilty only consumes more time and energy from you, and no one wins.

Balance comes when you are allowed to be extreme in the moment. Go all out while you're doing something. Guilt free. Worry free. You're at your best whenever you feel good about what you're doing. Give it all you've got when you're in the moment. Don't look behind or forward. Be all in.

We try so hard to fit so much into our lives. I wonder if we are even enjoying it. Going back to the journey, it almost seems like there's this invisible to-do list, and we must have one longer than our friends or colleagues so we can feel good about ourselves and never be deemed lazy.

Busy is seen as productive, whether it is or not. On the flip side, idle time is considered lazy. Gosh, has society really forced us to remove time to think or renew or rest? When does balance, not busy, become the goal?

CHAPTER 12: MOTIVATION

If at first you don't succeed, try again.

WHEN ARE WE GONNA START DANCING

Before the age of five, kids are limited in activities in which they can actually participate. At age three, there was so little my daughter could do. I was the parent scouring the Internet to find *something* to sign her up for. I wanted her to have lots of experiences, like a good mama should, right? She was still so little. Too young for camps. Too young for art school. Her options were limited to swim lessons and dance class.

I was talking with her day care principal about the lack of programs for a three-year-old, and here was her recommendation: "Start with the life skill. Which one will she use the rest of her life?"

So………. We chose dancing. Ha!

I ordered tiny leotards and ballet slippers and tap shoes. I picked up one of those cute bun wraps for her hair. She was ready for her first day of dance class.

I show up. I'm nervous. First child. First dance class. I'm scarred from watching *Dance Moms*. What was this going to be like? Piper, on the other hand, just smiled and said, "Let's go, Mama!" She looked so cute. She skipped from the car to the entrance to the dance studio.

Keep in mind dance parties are a regular at the Cook household. Piper has all kinds of moves. She loves to make up stuff and jump a lot. She especially likes floor moves where she rolls around and then finishes with some wild pose. She has great rhythm for her age. Dance class was going to be a blast!

Except it wasn't.

Parents are supposed to stay but not watch. There is a curtain dividing the waiting area and the dance floor. Every few seconds, here comes Piper around the curtain. "Can I have a hug?" she would ask. Well, of course. I just assume it is something new. New kiddos. New teacher. New stuff. She needs a little time to settle in. The teacher gives lollipops at the end of class to those who were good. Everyone gets a lollipop. All good. She just needed to adjust to the new thing.

Next class. Similar start. Keeps running over to me. Finally, the teacher convinces her to stay on the dance floor. About halfway through the class, they are working on plies and tendu steps, which I had to Google to spell correctly. These are dance moves that require very little movement, very little.

Piper stomps her foot and yells, "Teacher, when are we gonna start dancing? This is not dancing."

Oh geez.

The teacher puts her hands on her hips, and says in what seems like a French accent, "Well, my. This *IS* dancing."

I am ready for class to be over more than Piper. Somehow, Piper still gets a lollipop.

Next class. She stays on the dance floor. She doesn't ask about dancing. She is participating in the class. Then, all of a sudden, Piper goes over to the corner of the dance floor and sits down, criss-cross applesauce with her back facing the class. Well, huh.

I walk over to check on her. "Hey, pretty girl. Why are you sitting over here?"
"I'm mad."
"Why are you mad?"
"I just am."
"Do you wanna keep dancing?"
"I'm not dancing."

Finally, the teacher comes over to rescue me. Well, I thought she was going to rescue me. She looks at Piper and says, "Piper, if you are not going to join us today, I'm going to ask you to leave." What?!?! Ugh. Piper gets up and slinks back to the dance floor. She barely got a lollipop that day.

I asked her teachers at school if she'd been acting out or been difficult. Thankfully (for my sanity), they said she'd been normal and in fact, a good helper lately.

Hmmmm... what was going on?

Yep, Piper was bored. Her definition of dancing was wild and free and unstructured. Dance class was calm, polite, slow, and very structured.

According to her, they didn't even play fun music.

Last class for Piper (and mama). This was not the last class for the other girls. We were quitting.

Her last class was during the week of Halloween. They got to wear their costumes and dance freely to the *Monster Mash*. It was a great ending. They actually did dance, according to Piper. It was a great ending to something Mama had forced her baby girl to do a little too early.

In Piper's mind, she started and finished something, and there was a celebration at the end. I'll likely never tell her otherwise. (In reality, Mama set up her daughter to fail at the first thing she tried.)

What a "Mama Fail." Why was I forcing her to do something?

Unstructured play with a stack of boxes is just as good for her at the ripe age of three. Good Lord, I'm one of THOSE moms. Why do we feel compelled to give our kids "everything?"

Mamas, they don't need everything, and they definitely don't need some things too soon.

I should have taken the principal's advice and started with swim lessons.

Lesson learned.

If at first ~~you~~ don't succeed, try again.

If at first you don't succeed, find out why before you try again.

CHALLENGE: WAKE UP.

We lose motivation because daily life gets in the way. I want so badly to get up in the mornings to work out. I just have some brain block. I. Just. Can't. Do. It.

Why? Why can't I get my booty out of bed in the mornings? When I'm forced to get up early (like someone's bad dream or the dog barking), I feel more productive and like that I got up early. Why can my sleepy self not remember this?

Just like getting out of bed in the morning, you have to decide you're going to do it and create a system that reminds you to do it. Ha, I laugh at the Nike slogan "Just do it." Thanks, Captain Obvious. I just can't get over my mental block or duh, I would, dammit.

Permission granted to give these a try...

While I joked about getting out of bed in the morning in Chapter 1, the literal sense of "waking up" - my gosh, if you can do it, these steps are easy to knock out.

1. TWO MINUTES IS BETTER THAN 30 MINUTES.

Here's what I mean. When you know you have time, you don't use it quite as well. When you know you don't have enough time, you create a sense of urgency. You will get more done, have better focus, and knock out more tasks if you think you have less time than you do. This is scalable. For example, 30 minutes is better than 4 hours. Just one day is better than a week. It makes you get it done and not linger.

2. CREATE AN ENVIRONMENT FOR SUCCESS.

- Put your phone in the backseat so you're not distracted when you drive.
- Put your phone in the bathroom when you sleep to make you get up to get it.
- Put your phone on silent during dinner or any family time.

Seeing a pattern here?

- Prep time - if you have a goal, how much time is prepping versus doing? Take eating healthy, for example. Sunday Funday is a great way to get ready for the week. Play music, prep food with friends. Drink wine. Make it an event. Then you won't dread it so much.

3. PROMOTE UP.

Find an accountability partner that pushes you (preferably not a family member). It's also not Siri or Alexa. You need someone who is doing better than you are so you will be challenged and inspired by them. It's much harder to tell someone else no, especially someone who may have it together a little better than you do. Mamas, we are already pretty good at telling ourselves "No."

Part V:
Here We Go

CHAPTER 13: THINK

Seek and ye shall find.

Unicorns are Real...Sometimes

One warm spring day, Piper insisted on lying out in the sun. She's three. I assumed this doesn't usually happen until age fifteen, if you're lucky, which gives your beach trip some relaxation, but I digress. The sun was out, but the air was cool. Piper found a small sliver of deck where the sun shone. Then she disappeared. She came back with a bath towel and proceeded to take up the entire space that had sun.

She was on her belly, legs crossed up in the air and her chin on her hands. She stayed there for almost five minutes. I was amazed. What in the world was she thinking about? She was lost in thought, singing her own made-up song, looking out into the backyard, soaking up this particular day of spring.

I decided to do the same by just staring at her and smiling. I was making progress in her love of nature and her time without a screen. She loved being outside. Yay!

When she got up, I asked her what she was thinking about. She said, "Unicorns." In my happy voice, I said, "Oh, I love unicorns!" She darted her eyes at me and replied, "Mama, don't mock me. They are real." To her, they were just like Santa, the Easter Bunny, and the Tooth Fairy.

There's a sweet innocence in watching children play. There's an appreciation for all people and creatures when you are three. It's one that doesn't have any barriers, no limits.

When does it all change for us adults? I don't believe it's because we learn Santa was our parents. It happens much later. It happens when bad things happen, chipping away at our soul, making us not quite so innocent anymore.

Now the part of the story that completely ruins all of this sweetness is that after those five minutes she is ready to come inside and watch TV. When I said, "No," she fell to the kitchen floor doing the snow-angel move, wailing that I don't understand her, ever.

"You make me mad. I'm not happy with you right now. You don't wanna make me mad, Mama. And by the way, unicorns are NOT real. Don't be silly."

Ah. The sweet, innocent, unicorn-loving child has awoken back to her reality. I'm still thankful for those fleeting, simple five minutes. Even a three-year-old can figure out how to give herself five minutes.

Thinking is hard. We are so bombarded by information, real or not, it's hard for us to focus long enough to absorb what's coming our way. Would you believe our attention span is only eight seconds?[9] That's down from twelve seconds just ten years ago? At what point are we at zero and, *thwalpck*, (in the voice of a robot), "ONE SECOND. I MUST INJECT MYSELF WITH THINKING SERUM SO I CAN CONTINUE THIS CONVERSATION WITH YOU."

Sound ridiculous? Watch *Black Mirror* on Netflix, and then see what you think.

We can't absorb as much as before. We don't read anymore. We're worried about third graders reading to learn as opposed to learning to read? Hell, we don't even read as adults! Think about it. Do you read the instructions that come with a new gadget? No, you search for a YouTube video that shows you how to do it. You avoided reading and comprehending!

The communications world is proving that, too. We must use headline clickbait or outrageous claims to get you to look. Then, we must bold words and bullet the entire article so you can catch the gist of it. That's all people can absorb, so you better not write any more than that.

Now pause. If you have made it this far in this book, congratulate yourself and keep going. The best is at the end. Just don't flip there yet, even though you likely already have!

Being concise is good. Being wordy is bad. Being a thinker is good. Only skimming is bad.

Blinkist shares a summary for thousands of books you don't have time to read. Is that good or bad?

Google is the ultimate real-time library. Is that good or bad?

Not to rehash the journey and time chapters, but we are *actively* shortening our journey which should give us *more* time to think. Why is that not happening? We're more frazzled than ever!

Seek and Xe shall find.

Unplug to recharge.

CHALLENGE: RELEASE WILDLY.

What are we so afraid of? Why can't we let anyone know we're human? As mamas, we won't talk about fails, yet we're oh-so-quick to offer unsolicited advice. Who are we? We're so afraid someone will tell us we're doing something wrong that we shortchange ourselves from truly learning. Don't we want to instill a desire to learn in our children? Of course we do! Release wildly with books. Do we want our children to have inspirational experiences where they push themselves to do something that seems impossible? Of course we do! Release wildly with creative thoughts and critical thinking.

Why are we so resistant to release wildly ourselves? The only wild releases we're doing probably have something negative to do with them or some crazy moment we've built up. It's just a spew. Not inspirational.

We have to get back to a world where we think for ourselves. An easy answer can't always be at our fingertips. We must develop critical thinking skills, and if we're not doing it and showing this to our kiddos as examples, then how in the world are they going to get it?

Why don't we allow ourselves to do what we want our children to do? We should lead the way for them. Release wildly, and you will.

Permission granted to give these a try...

1. AFTERNOON THINKING.

Structure your day so you get the most out of it. You're going to check more off your list from the time you wake up until lunch. After that, your brain wants a nap, and we don't get naps as adults. Well, other countries actually have napping centers because they see the value of a break – but not Americans, there's no time for that.[10] Then again, we are seeing a major shift in innovative companies, like Google, so maybe there's hope.

Reserve the afternoon, if at all possible, for thinking time. You are more prone to think outside the box when your mind is tired. You're going to be less productive anyway. Might as well try and solve a problem that's been lingering.

2. ACCEPT CRAZY IDEAS.

Do you think people thought Uber was crazy when that idea first came about? Of course! Twenty years ago, if someone had said their business idea was to seek out strangers to drive you around, they would have been mocked. That's innovation today. Think tanks exist because we need a space for thoughtful thinking. Just make sure when you're thinking crazy, it's about adding value to our lives in a way that's good for us.

3. CREATE UNSTRUCTURED ADULT PLAY.

Go to one of those canvas painting places and drink or chat with friends while you paint. I think adults need unstructured play as much as brain-absorbing-everything-they-see kiddos. Or simply sit outside and do nothing. Enough about that. Just go do that.

CHAPTER 14: CONNECTION

Absence makes the heart grow fonder.

You Have a Lot of Homework

Absence versus presence. Being present all the time doesn't make you engaged. Being absent may mean you're focused on something that needs your full attention, and that's not bad. It's about *when* you choose to be absent or present.

Are we making connections built on where we are each day, based on our four rooms (physical, mental, emotional, and spiritual)? Or are we very disconnected?

Physical presence does not count. You must be fully engaged to reach people today. If you're on the iPad at a soccer game and your kiddo looks up at you looking down, ouch. In this moment, physical presence alone doesn't count. An opportunity to connect with your kiddo is gone.

My daughter answered questions one day in class that were then turned into a Mother's Day gift.

The project was called "All About Mom" and here's how it went, noting the underlined words are the ones my daughter filled in.

Let me tell you about my mom. My mom is 16 years old. The best thing she cooks is ham. Her favorite food is chicken. Her favorite thing to do is go to Walmart. We like to watch TV together. She is really good at reading, and she likes to do homework a lot. As you can see, my mom is special because she is special to me.

Here's what I gathered from my Mother's Day gift:

- I look younger than I am! Win!
- I need to cook more.
- We watch too much TV.
- I go to Walmart so often it now seems like I like it.
- I clearly work too much since she deduced, at age four, that I have a lot of homework. :(

I need to be more present. I was trying to "mom so hard" the right way, and I still didn't realize how much time I was not engaged with my own daughter. As a working mom, I have about five hours with my daughter each day during the week. That's about an hour and a half in the mornings while getting ready. Then on a good day, I have from 5:29 p.m. - 9:00 p.m., with nearly an hour of that figuring out how to get her to go to bed. Now remember, the bedtime process begins around 7:30 p.m. That's not much time.

I pride myself on making people feel special. I even train others how to do it, and I still didn't notice I wasn't living up to my own standards, my own mantra.

Thomas Friedman, best-selling author, said, "We used to work with our hands. Now, we have machines. Then we had to use our brains. Now, we have technology. The only thing left is to use our hearts."[11] I'm excited about a generation working personally and professionally with love in mind. The auto-decision world is already happening. You really don't have to think about much anymore. It's why the journey is being shortened. You get the answer quicker, and you don't see a need to know why.

We must discern where presence is valuable and where it is detrimental. I also think we are building a culture based on fake loyalty. For example, there is a fake sense of connection that exists with rewards programs. I'm a Marriott and Delta member, and I'm only as "loved" as I am "loyal." Loyalty is calculated based upon how much money I've spent with them.

Connections must be real. Connections matter if they are real.

Absence m~~ak~~es the heart grow fonder.

Presence is what the heart needs.

CHALLENGE: BE IN THE RIGHT PLACE.

Showing up is more than half the battle. The bigger question is, where are you showing up?

As long as you're showing up to the right place, you'll be okay. Think about sitting in an unproductive meeting. How do you feel? Are you present or drifting away? Why aren't you present? Now, think beyond a meeting. How often are you on your phone when your kid gets home from school? How many times must you divide your attention when you're with the family? Is it a healthy dose of divided attention or not?

How can we work to create minor moments of connectivity that lead to major real connections?

Permission granted to give these a try...

1. SEND RANDOM NICE NOTES TO PEOPLE.

Start a mini goal: 1/week

Think about how nice it is to receive a kind note from someone else. We've all heard it's better to give than receive. Do this small thing to make you feel good about making someone else's day. Even a simple text is a good start. And, it's worth it.

2. LOOK PEOPLE IN THE EYE.

Don't you hate it when you're at a social gathering and someone keeps darting his or her eyes away to see who else is in the room? Super annoying. It makes you feel like they don't care what you're saying, only who they think they need to get to next. Isn't it refreshing when someone seems like they are paying attention to you, actively listening by looking at you? Yes, eye contact matters.

3. FAKE IS FATAL.

Stop believing that social media connections are real connections. They are, at best, happy acquaintances. At worst, they're making you depressed about your own life. You already intuitively know this. Build your relationships in real life. This doesn't mean you can't have strong long-distance relationships. It just means that you don't need Facebook friends to make you feel better or give you a false security that people care. Here's a good way to gauge this. How many people tell you Happy Birthday *not* on Facebook? That takes extra effort. Facebook friends get a prompt to do it. Which is better? Real is better. Don't be more popular on Facebook than you are in real life.

CHAPTER 15: EXCEED EXPECTATIONS

Never look a gift horse in the mouth.

PIPER IS READY

Piper comes full circle.

Every morning, Piper crawls in bed with me before it's time to get going for the day. Typically, it's the normal struggle. She's not ready to get up. She's not ready to go to school. "It's a school day? I don't like school days!" This leads to her screaming, "I. Don't. Like. School. Days." So much for those last precious minutes of snuggling.

Piper asks almost every night at bedtime whether tomorrow is a school day or a home day. There's not good or bad association with either, she just asks. Sometimes, she's excited it's a school day and other days, she's highly disappointed. Sometimes, she's thrilled it's a home day, and sometimes, she questions if we are right, because she really wants a school day.

Piper was visiting with her godparents one day. She asked them whether or not it was a school or home day, and they replied, "A school day."

Piper looked at them, hung her head, shaking and said, "School day after school day breaks my bones." They couldn't help but laugh. I tell this story because it speaks to the chances of Piper getting up and doing anything we ask of her on her own.

Then, this one morning happened. When snuggle time was over, she hopped out of bed and went to her room. This particular morning, it was *me* not ready to get up. I rolled over and must have gone back to sleep. We call this forbidden sleep at our house. The best kind that always leaves a twinge of guilt.

In my half-asleep state, I hear Piper run down the hallway. Huh. That's odd. In a few minutes, she comes back. She's fully clothed, shoes and all.

She states, to no one in particular, "I'm ready to go to school. I let Sophie outside and gave her a treat. I brushed my teeth. I'm ready." What?!?! I must still be dreaming. The shock on my face was pure astonishment.

Without thinking, I looked at her puzzled and asked, "Piper, why are you ready?"

Dammit. Missed opportunity to praise. Missed opportunity to connect.

What I should have done was pause, and then say, "Way to go, lady! You're awesome." Who cares that it's 5:15 a.m., and you will have to wait at least two hours before we can even drop you off at school? I should have instantly praised her for the eight things she did on her own that usually take begging, coaxing, bribing, and more.

Moment exceeded for her. Moment wasted for me.

She exceeded my expectations. I want to exceed hers, too.

Never look a ~~gift~~ horse in the mouth.

Give better than Grandma.

CHALLENGE: Adios Average.

This chapter is last because it is the most meaningful to me. Permission granted to GO BIG on an ending.

I've always gravitated toward leaders, wanting to seek out mentors. Many might say it's because I didn't have a mama present, and I need to replace that feeling a mother should provide. I've been fortunate to surround myself with great people. It's the main reason I feel confident enough to go chase my dreams AND have a great family. Papaw is my number one mentor. He rarely told me a lesson. He showed me countless lessons through his own actions. I'm just glad I was watching.

The other mentor I really watched was a gentleman who left this world way too early. He taught me how to exceed expectations in the littlest of ways. In his mind, it was simple and significantly important. It was his mantra. He left this world leaving an indelible mark, and the entire community lives and breathes "Exceeding Expectations" to carry on his legacy.

Whoever your mentors and cheerleaders are, believe them. They know you can exceed expectations.

I sure hope I have.

Permission granted to give these a try...

1. SURPRISE OTHERS

I love surprises - especially those I know about, so I know how to react. (Anybody with me?)

Here are a few memorable ones for me.

I had been working at my internship for a few weeks, and it was Friday. All of a sudden, my boss (mentor mentioned) walked in with breakfast for everyone. Yay! Surprise. You never knew when you would get a free breakfast, and it was always fun when you saw him walk in with a big bag. Breakfast is easy. The reward he got from doing it was the reason he did it.

I have a recurring lunch date with three amazing ladies. They are pioneering leaders with wisdom oozing from them. One of these ladies, is my mentor's lovely wife. She lives "Exceeding Expectations" every day. At one of our lunches, it was her birthday. Do you know what she did on HER birthday? She brought *US* a gift, a book that inspired her. She gave a gift instead of receiving one. In her mind, that was still a gift to herself.

My Papaw is full of surprises, too. When I used to dance at a theme park, we would go out as a group to eat after a show. It tickled him to secretly pay the bill, and no one knew it was him. The waitress would come to the table, and someone would say, "We are ready for our checks, and do you mind to split us up?" The waitress would smile and say, "It's been taken care of." After many of these, and with Papaw being the only one smiling and not shocked, people came to realize it was him who had taken care of the entire bill. He loved that. The joy he got out of giving was way better than the surprise others got from receiving a free dinner.

My husband is the best at spurts of "Exceeding Expectations." In an effort not to make anyone roll their eyes at the sappiness, I'll briefly mention a couple. On Valentine's Day, it was just a normal work day. I had several meetings out of the office and then, like always, we would stay in. He would cook dinner, and we would watch *The Notebook*. Yes, this *one* night he would give in. We're on the go so much it's nice to have a peaceful evening at home.

Much to my surprise, he had planned more than our normal dinner and a movie. He had a rose delivered with a note to every place I went that day, every meeting, at lunch, and even when I took the dog to the groomer! To say I blushed was an understatement. The planning to pull that off was the most flattering part. I thought he never looked at our calendar!

Another time was Mother's Day Week. Yes, ladies - not just Mother's Day. Each day, there was a new room cleaned, a cocktail waiting for me when I got home, and dinner served by my husband. It was a week about me. He handled everything, and I got to relax.

Now, before you tune me out because this is disgustingly romantic, let me let you in on a secret. The reason I got Mother's Day Week was because my husband forgot Mother's Day the year before. This makes us real. Had he always loved me? Of course. Did he feel bad about forgetting? Horribly. His effort to correct shows his true nature.

What are you doing to work on the relationships in your life? Think about it. Are you "Exceeding Expectations?" If not, don't expect awesomeness from anyone. It starts with you.

2. SURPRISE YOUR WORLD.

Give to something bigger than yourself. It's so much more rewarding. If you think no one deserves it, well there's an even better reason to try. (Rise above, mamas.) We all love to hear heartwarming stories where altruism is at work, goodness at work.

I live in Kingsport, Tennessee, and Tennessee is the Volunteer State. Kingsport is known for the intangible "Kingsport Spirit," so maybe, I come by it naturally. Our city is full of people exceeding expectations for no other reason than to be a part of something special and bigger than themselves.

Here are some quick ideas to get you started if you think you're not up for the challenge of being nice to people quite yet.

- Pick up trash. Make a city beautiful, one piece of trash at a time.
- Paint a rock. Go leave it in a park for someone else to find.
- Leave clothes for the homeless on a fence downtown.
- Make cookies, and give them away to brighten someone's day.

Answer the question you know they are asking. How many times do we purposefully answer the exact question we are asked because someone didn't ask it the right way? What a jerk move. Disney never does that.[12] (Kingsport doesn't do that either.) If someone were to ask what time the three o'clock parade is, a Disney cast member would say, "The parade starts by the castle, and I would make sure to find a good spot around 2:45 p.m. so you don't miss anything!" Why can't we offer this type of answer to others?

These are just a few examples of what we can do to exceed expectations. Find a way to give back to the world, your community, your family, and yourself.

3. Surprise yourself.

Permission granted to be good to yourself. And then, every once in a while, GO BIG. Accept the challenge to push yourself, take a risk, take a break, get a massage, close the door and leave kids in another room. The possibilities are endless and evolving. Just make sure you're paying attention to what you need. After you've taken care of that, go do something you want.

Everyone benefits from a happy mama.

What a nice book ending. We started with Piper refusing to put on clothes to go to school and ended with her exceeding expectations and completing all morning chores (some not even assigned to her) before I got out of bed. Both instances are simply moments in time where we cry and cheer. All experiences, even tiny, are moments in time. Good ones never last long enough, and bad ones seem to linger. Either way, they are moments in time.

You have these same moments in your life. If you look at the journey in this book, it moves from "I'm overwhelmed" to "Here we go." We can't say we won't have a journey that takes twists and turns or has ups and downs. Life is all over these chapters. Some moments are instant. Some are daily. Some last years, and some last forever. Wherever you are on your journey, whichever one that may be, I hope you can find motivation, solace, and a little bit of laughter as you work to reach your fullest potential.

Permission Granted. Go Be a Better You. It's Time.

You're Welcome, Mama.

Notes

1. Bush, L., Cravalho, A., House, R., Jackson, C., & Scherziner, N. "Where You Are." Moana. Espino, M., Foa'i, O., Mancina, M., Miranca, L., & Page, A. Walt Disney Records. 19 Nov. 2016.

2. Pink, Daniel H. *When: The Scientific Secrets of Perfect Timing*. Riverhead Books, 2018.

3.Queenan, Joe. "Neuro-Logic: How Your Brain Is Keeping You from Changing Your Mind." *The Rotarian*, May 2018, pp. 38-43.

4. Cron, Ian. "Are You Self Aware?" Leadercast Live 2018, 4 May 2018, Atlanta, GA, Kingsport Simulcast.

5. Mann, Derek T. Y., and Martin Delahoussaye. "Personality Style at Work: Core Profile Info Kit." *Personality Style at Work Assessment*, HRDQ, 2018, www.hrdqstore.com.

6. Ward, Kate. *Personality Style at Work: The Secret To Working With (Almost) Anyone*. McGraw Hill, 2012.

7. Schwantes, Marcel. "Why Are Your Employees Quitting? A Study Says It Comes Down to Any of These 6 Reasons." Inc.com, Leadership From the Core, 23 Oct. 2017, www.inc.com/marcel-schwantes/why-are-your-employees-quitting-a-study-says-it-comes-down-to-any-of-these-6-reasons.html.

8. Chaykowski, Kathleen. "Facebook's Latest Algorithm Change: Here Are The News Sites That Stand to Lose The Most." *Forbes*, 31 Mar. 2018.

9. McSpadden, Kevin. "You Now Have a Shorter Attention Span Than a Goldfish." *Time*, 14 May 2015. www.time.com.

10. Channick, Robert. "Office Napping Climbs Out from Under the Desk and into High-Tech Pods." *Chicago Tribune*, 5 July 2018. www.chicagotribune.com.

11. Friedman, Thomas. "The Big Trends Shaping the World Today and Impacting Our Community." Connect Knox, 15 Feb. 2018, Knoxville Convention Center.

12. Jones, Bruce. "How Disney Encourages Employees to Deliver Exceptional Customer Service." *Harvard Business Review*, 28 Feb. 2018. Sponsor Content from Disney Institute.

Made in the USA
Middletown, DE
30 November 2018